small plates perfect wines

Creating Little Dishes with Big Flavors

Lori Lyn Narlock

**Andrews McMeel
Publishing, LLC**
Kansas City

07 08 09 10 11 SDB 10 9 8 7 6 5 4 3 2 1

ISBN-13: 978-0-7407-6913-9

ISBN-10: 0-7407-6913-8

Library of Congress Control Number: 2007927688

Concept, packaging, and design: Jennifer Barry Design, Fairfax, California

Layout production: Kristen Hall
Recipe testing: Kate Washington
Food and prop styling: Kim Konecny, assisted by Julia Scahill
Copyediting: Carolyn Miller
Proofreading: Beverly McGuire
Indexing: Ken Dellapenta

www.andrewsmcmeel.com

Attention: Schools and Businesses
Andrews McMeel books are available at quantity discounts with
bulk purchase for educational, business, or sales promotional use.
For information, please write to:
Special Sales Department, Andrews McMeel Publishing, LLC,
4520 Main Street, Kansas City, Missouri 64111.

contents

introduction

Good wine, food, and camaraderie —if you have all three, you have the makings for a great meal.

—Randy Ullom, Kendall-Jackson winemaker

Small plates are revolutionizing the way we eat. From restaurants to homes, dynamic menus composed of small plates are being served in lieu of traditional one-plate entrées. Made for sharing, small plates can easily be served alone as an appetizer or first course, but are even better when combined with other small plates as a complete meal.

Small plates are inspired by the tapas of Spain, the antipasti of Italy, the meze of the Middle East, the yakitori of Japan, and a myriad of other little dishes from cuisines around the globe. What these traditional foods all share in common is the ritual of relaxing with something to eat and a glass of wine from the same place, from sherry to sake.

The small plates showcased in this book invite you to the table to mark the break between work and play, to enjoy a glass of wine, and to savor your meal in the company of others. Peruse the recipes to whet your appetite, then step into the kitchen and start cooking. With these small-plates recipes in hand, you are already on your way to a great meal.

small plates, wine country style

Small plates are a great way to play with new combinations of ingredients to pair with delicious wines.

— Justin Wangler, Kendall-Jackson executive chef

It's not a surprise that where you find good wine you'll find good food. At Kendall-Jackson's Wine Center, in the heart of Sonoma County's bountiful wine country, this is especially true. Jess Jackson, Kendall-Jackson's founder, is committed to promoting the marriage of wine and food and to that end has created a slice of culinary heaven amid the lush vineyards of Sonoma.

At the helm is Justin Wangler, Kendall-Jackson's executive chef, who it can easily be argued has a dream job: He works for a man who shares his passion for food in a location surrounded by Mother Nature's bounty with a team of talented individuals. The Kendall-Jackson culinary team, including chefs Andrei Livinenko and Matthew Lowe, are ambassadors of the pleasures of food and wine. They spend their days introducing Wine Center visitors to dishes created especially for enjoying with wine.

For this book, the Kendall-Jackson culinary team collected its favorite small-plates recipes, many of which were developed to take advantage of the abundance of fantastic ingredients available in the wine country, especially those grown in the Wine Center's two-plus acres of gardens.

Paradise as Inspiration

In the same way that nature's beauty inspires artists, the gardens at Kendall-Jackson supply the culinary team with their own palette of colors, flavors, textures, and aromas to use in creating gourmet masterpieces. The gardens actually consist of several smaller gardens, each dedicated to showcasing the beauty of flora and food. All are farmed using sustainable techniques that encourage diversity, such as planting heirloom seeds and creating areas to attract butterflies and beneficial pests.

The Wine Sensory Gardens are a unique section composed of a broad variety of plants that represent the various aromas and flavors you might detect in a glass of wine. The garden is divided into sections that correspond with red, white, and specific wine varietals, with each section featuring plants with the aromas and flavors found in the corresponding wines. It's easy to imagine Kendall-Jackson's chefs trekking through the garden for ideas when it's time to develop a recipe for a specific wine. From citrus to raspberries, there's a little bit of the sensory gardens in the recipes throughout this book.

Even more crucial to the creativity of the culinary team are the Culinary Gardens. To tour the neat rows of both familiar and exotic plants is a treat for gardeners and food lovers alike, as well as a virtual exploration of the riches of Sonoma County. The culinary garden itself is divided into smaller sections, including areas devoted to specific countries and cultures, among them France, Italy, Asia, and South America. Its unparalleled bounty offers the chefs fresh, at-the-peak-of-their-season ingredients. From peppery arugula and spicy cilantro to juicy plums and sweet persimmons, the garden's abundant harvest is the foundation for this book's diverse recipes.

The most well-known ingredient that grows in the Wine Center's gardens is the heirloom tomatoes, the cornerstone of Kendall-Jackson's Heirloom Tomato Festival, held every September. Now in its second decade, the festival is testament to the winery's devotion to all things delicious. Every year, the gardens are filled with more than two thousand tomato lovers, who come to taste the nearly two hundred heirloom varieties at their most delicious.

Showcasing It All in Small Plates

From the herbs showcased in the French Garden to the spices of the South American Garden, from spring's fava beans and summer's squash to fall's persimmons and winter's cauliflower, you'll find the gardens' influence in every recipe in this book. Each small plate and every wine it's paired with are a reflection of the diverse and delicious bounty of the California wine country. Use this book to inspire your own gardening plans or excursions to your local farmers' market and produce counters, then re-create these food and wine pairings at your table. Enjoy!

dynamic matches: pairing and serving wine

You want to have fun—plain and simple.

—Randy Ullom, Kendall-Jackson winemaker

Pairing Wine and Food

Never has there been better advice for pairing wine and food than just to enjoy yourself. Eating and drinking should be all about pleasure, not work. Besides, hypothetically there's no perfect wine for food. Blasphemy? No, not really, because the enjoyment of wine and food separately and together is so subjective. What one person may love, the person across the table may hate.

That said, there are some matches between wine and food that are unanimously considered sublime and others that just don't work. To achieve the former and avoid the latter, the tastemakers at Kendall-Jackson offer a few guiding principles to make pairing simple and foolproof.

The most important factor is balance. What does this mean? In food, there should be a balance between the acid, salt, spice, bitterness, richness, and other components that make up the taste of a dish. When a dish is in balance, it will make a great match with any wine. For example, at Kendall-Jackson, there is a bounty of beautiful fruit available for the culinary team to use in the kitchen. In general, most fruit is sweet, which can make wine taste bitter, but when that fruit is part of a salad balanced by a tangy vinaigrette, some peppery greens, and rich nuts, the result is a balanced dish that will pair beautifully with any wine, red or white.

What happens to wine when food isn't balanced? It depends. Here are a few possible scenarios:

- Sweet foods can make a dry wine taste bitter, because the tannins are emphasized and the fruit flavors become masked.
- Acidic foods can make a wine taste flat and dull, because the acid in the wine is masked.
- Bitter foods can give wine an off taste, because it overpowers the fruit flavors.
- Spicy foods can make a wine taste bitter, because the spice emphasizes the wine's tannins.

The aim is to match food and wine with the same kind of intensity so that neither overpowers the other. Great matches share similar traits.

Here are some examples of wine and food that share a similar intensity:

- Creamy Chardonnay and buttery crab
- Crisp Sauvignon Blanc and tangy goat cheese
- Earthy Pinot Noir and mushrooms
- Fruity Merlot and robust lamb
- Late harvest wines and port and sweet desserts

Conversely, sometimes you need contrast. Great matches can be made between wine and food that complement each other.

Here are some classic examples of wine and food pairings that capitalize on contrast:

- Slightly sweet Riesling is a great match for dishes that contain chiles as an ingredient.
- Fruity Chardonnay is the perfect foil for a pungent blue cheese.
- Jammy Zinfandel provides just the right counterpoint to a food that's naturally bitter, like radicchio or Brussels sprouts.

When in doubt, play it safe. Chardonnay and Pinot Noir are irresistible to wine and food lovers alike. And with good reason, as they both offer a lovely balance between fresh-fruit flavors and a gentle acidity that makes them especially food-friendly.

And finally, eat and drink what you like. You can never go wrong if you like both the wine and the food. Experiment with your preferences. You never know what great matches you'll discover.

Wine Varietals and Small-Plates Pairings at a Glance

Sauvignon Blanc

Profile: Light and crisp, with citrus, fig, and hints of tropical fruit

Best matches: Dishes with a lively acidity from citrus or vinegar, such as:

> Rock Shrimp, Citrus, and Fennel Salad (page 15)
>
> Mediterranean Cucumber Salad (page 22)
>
> Lemon-Chicken Kebabs with Moroccan Herb Sauce
> (page 83)

Chardonnay

Profile: Buttery and lush with hints of toasty oak wrapped in tropical fruit and crisp apple flavors

Best matches: Dishes with a subtle richness from nuts, aioli, mayonnaise, or creamy cheeses, such as:

> Caramelized Pear and Walnut Salad with Prosciutto
> (page 28)
>
> Fennel and Gorgonzola Gratin (page 48)
>
> Capellini with Clams (page 75)

Riesling

Profile: Nearly dry, with apricot, pear, and orange blossom flavors

Best matches: Dishes with fruit, cheese, or spicy ingredients, such as:

> Peach Salad with Arugula, Bacon, and Mint (page 27)
>
> Curry-Dusted Halibut with Arugula and Jasmine Rice
> (page 63)
>
> Grilled Pork with Plum Salsa (page 84)

Muscat Canelli

Profile: Off-dry, with citrus flavors mingling with peach blossom notes and spices

Best matches: Dishes with a defined sweet component or a fiery essence, such as:

> Molasses-Almond Shrimp on Spicy Cabbage Salad
> (page 60)
>
> Mini Summer Squash Cupcakes with Lemon Glaze (page 122)
>
> Plum Crostadas (page 118)

Late Harvest Chardonnay

Profile: Voluptuous and sweet with candied pear, honeycomb, and stone fruit flavors

Best matches: Desserts made with fresh and dried fruit and nuts, such as:

> Mini Summer Squash Cupcakes with Lemon Glaze (page 122)
>
> Plum Crostadas (page 118)
>
> Caramel Nut Tartlets (page 127)

Rosé

Profile: Crisp and lush at the same time, with soft berry flavors

Best matches: Dishes with a little spice and/or a little richness, such as:

> Chilled Corn Soup with Meyer Lemon Olive Oil (page 40)
>
> Crab Salad with Rémoulade (page 68)
>
> Paprika-Spiced Grilled Calamari with Cannellini Beans
> (page 71)

Pinot Noir

Profile: Silky, with cherry and strawberry flavors mingled with smoky earth tones

Best matches: Dishes with beef, or meaty ingredients like mushrooms and eggplant, such as:

Grilled Eggplant and Tomatoes (page 39)

Golden Chanterelle–Topped Crostini (page 47)

Seared Steak with Mushroom Pan Sauce (page 91)

Merlot

Profile: Smooth tannins surrounded by cherry, plum, and raspberry flavors and hints of chocolate

Best matches: Dishes with intensely flavored ingredients like balsamic vinegar, lamb, and eggplant, such as:

Balsamic-Glazed Potatoes and Onions (page 51)

Grilled Eggplant–Red Pepper Rolls (page 44)

Lamb-Filled Roasted Onions (page 100)

Zinfandel

Profile: Bursting with sweet berry flavors and hints of pepper and spices

Best matches: Dishes with bold-flavored ingredients, such as:

Ratatouille with Summer Herbs (page 43)

Roasted Cauliflower with Braised Radicchio (page 56)

Pepper Salami Skewers with Wine-Poached Olives and Figs (page 92)

Syrah

Profile: Rich and robust, with black cherry, currant, and pepper flavors and notes of smokiness

Best matches: Dishes with a peppery essence and robustly flavored ingredients, such as:

Roasted Brussels Sprouts with Chorizo (page 52)

Flank Steak with Pepper Crust (page 87)

Duck and Spinach Empanadas with Persimmon Chutney (page 102)

Cabernet Sauvignon

Profile: Full-bodied, with black currant, coffee, and dark chocolate notes surrounded by dark fruit flavors

Best matches: Robust, intensely flavored dishes, such as:

Grilled Beef Tenderloin and Heirloom Tomato Skewers (page 88)

Braised Chicken with Swiss Chard (page 108)

Bite-Size Brownies with Chocolate-Cabernet Glaze (page 126)

Meritage

Profile: Layers of flavors, including pomegranate, dark chocolate, and espresso, enveloped by firm tannins and a smooth texture

Best matches: Dishes with a smokiness from grilled or roasted ingredients, such as:

Grilled Beef Tenderloin and Heirloom Tomato Skewers (page 88)

Seared Steak with Mushroom Pan Sauce (page 91)

Dark Chocolate Truffles (page 125)

Port

Profile: Rich, complex, and sweet with dark fruit flavors

Best matches: Great with sweet desserts made with chocolate, nuts, and spices, such as:

Bite-Size Brownies with Chocolate-Cabernet Glaze (page 126)

Warm Chocolate Puddle Cakes (page 113)

Wine-Serving Tips

- One 750-ml bottle equals six 4-ounce glasses
- Plan for 1 glass of each wine per person during a dinner party (about 1 bottle of each wine)
- If possible, offer a different glass for each varietal (or for whites and reds)
- Serve white wine cool but not cold for the best flavor
- Serve red wine slightly cooler than room temperature
- Chill a bottle of wine quickly by immersing it in ice and water
- Decant a wine 30 minutes before serving to bring it up to room temperature or to expose to air
- Recork leftover wine and store in the refrigerator for drinking or cooking with later

Serving Wine with Small-Plates Menus

The beauty of small-plates menus is the variety of flavors introduced with each new dish, resulting in the opportunity to pair one meal with a range of wines. You can serve the wine suggested for each recipe, or you can pick your favorite varietal and serve it with every dish, or you can select a couple of different wines and let each person decide what he or she wants to drink. Remember, this is about enjoying yourself, so have fun.

- Serve a red and a white. It's okay to go back and forth between red and white wines when you're eating. If you're using the same glass, you can rinse your glass with water or with a little bit of the new wine, but unless you are switching from a sweet wine to a dry wine, this isn't really necessary.
- Set all of the wines out at once. Wines change as they sit open and are exposed to air. With a little bit of oxygen, and sometimes a warm room temperature, wines will change while sitting in your glass, which could also change how they taste paired with the food. This also offers everyone the opportunity to decide which wines they like best with which dishes and to test whether or not those matches stay the same throughout the meal.
- Start with small pours. If you plan on serving more than one wine varietal, offer 2 to 3 ounces to each guest when a new wine is served. (You can figure out how much this is by pouring ¼ or ⅓ cup of water into a similar glass and noting where the fill line is.)

salads

In a medium bowl, combine half of the lemon zest, half of the lemon juice, and 1 tablespoon of the flavored or extra-virgin olive oil. Add the shrimp, toss to coat, and let stand for 30 minutes.

Cut the skin from the orange, following the curve of the fruit with the knife. Carefully cut the sections from the membranes, working over a bowl to catch any juice. Put the orange segments in a separate bowl. Measure the juice; if less than 2 tablespoons, add enough juice to make 2 tablespoons. Add the remaining lemon zest, remaining lemon juice, remaining 1 tablespoon flavored or extra-virgin olive oil, and the shallots to the orange juice.

Using a mandoline or a sharp knife, cut the fennel into very thin crosswise slices. Lightly chop the reserved fennel fronds. Add the fennel, fronds, and orange juice mixture to the bowl with the orange segments and toss gently to coat. Season with salt and pepper to taste.

In a large nonstick skillet, heat the 1 tablespoon olive oil over high heat until it shimmers but is not smoking. Add the shrimp and sauté until pink on both sides, about 3 minutes. Using a slotted spoon, transfer the shrimp to the fennel mixture. Divide among 6 small bowls and serve immediately.

rock shrimp, citrus, and fennel salad

Serves 6

2 teaspoons grated lemon zest

¼ cup freshly squeezed lemon juice

2 tablespoons Meyer lemon olive oil or extra-virgin olive oil

1 pound shelled rock shrimp

1 orange

2 tablespoons freshly squeezed orange juice (if needed)

2 tablespoons minced shallots

2 fennel bulbs, trimmed and cored (reserve fennel fronds)

Kosher salt and freshly ground black pepper

1 tablespoon olive oil

Wine pairing: Sauvignon Blanc

warm potato and fava bean salad

Serves 6

6 new potatoes (about 1¾ pounds total), unpeeled

    and quartered

5 tablespoons olive oil

Grated zest and juice of 1 lemon

Kosher salt and freshly ground black pepper

1 pound fava beans, shelled, or 1 cup frozen shelled soybeans

1 shallot, minced

3 loosely packed cups watercress leaves (about 3 bunches)

1 large piece pecorino cheese for shaving

Wine pairing: Chardonnay

Preheat the oven to 375°F. In a medium bowl, combine the potatoes, 3 tablespoons of the olive oil, the lemon zest, and juice. Spread on a baking sheet and sprinkle generously with salt and pepper. Bake, stirring occasionally, until golden brown and tender, 30 to 35 minutes.

In a large pot of salted boiling water, blanch the fava beans for 1 minute. Drain in a colander and rinse under cold water to stop the cooking. Peel the skins from the beans and discard the skins. (If using soybeans, cook them in a large pot of salted boiling water until tender, about 5 minutes. Drain.)

In a medium bowl, whisk together the shallot and the remaining 2 tablespoons olive oil. Season with salt and pepper to taste. Add the watercress and toss to coat.

Divide the watercress among 6 small plates. Top each serving with 4 potato quarters and equal amounts of fava beans. Using a vegetable peeler, shave a few slices of pecorino over each salad. Serve warm.

Preheat the oven to 400°F. Lay two large pieces of aluminum foil in the shape of an X on a baking sheet. Place the beets in the center and drizzle with 2 tablespoons of the olive oil. Gather the foil into a packet and crimp to seal.

Bake until the beets are tender when pierced with a sharp knife, 40 to 60 minutes. Remove from the oven and let cool.

Meanwhile, combine the dates, cumin, and fennel in a small saucepan. Add water to cover and bring to a boil over medium heat. Cook for 10 minutes. Drain, reserving the liquid, and let the dates cool to the touch. Peel the skin from the dates, remove and reserve the pits, and chop the dates.

In a blender, combine the dates, vinegar, pomegranate molasses, 2 tablespoons of the reserved cooking liquid, and the reserved date pits. Puree until smooth. With the machine running, gradually add the remaining 2 tablespoons olive oil in a slow, steady stream. Add more reserved cooking liquid to thin if desired. Season with salt and pepper to taste.

Pour a little of the vinaigrette in the center of each of 6 small plates. Arrange some of the beets on top, dividing equally between each portion. Garnish with the chives and serve.

Note: Pomegranate molasses is available at Middle Eastern markets and most grocery stores alongside maple syrups.

beet salad with tangy date vinaigrette
Serves 6

2 pounds small beets, greens trimmed to 1 inch

4 tablespoons olive oil

4 Medjool dates

½ teaspoon cumin seeds

½ teaspoon fennel seeds

2 tablespoons sherry vinegar

1 tablespoon pomegranate molasses

Kosher salt and freshly ground black pepper

1 tablespoon chopped fresh chives, for garnish

Wine pairing: Pinot Noir

green beans with lemon vinaigrette, blue cheese, and almonds

In a large pot of salted boiling water, cook the green beans until tender, 2 to 3 minutes. Drain in a colander and rinse with cold water to stop the cooking. Set aside.

For the vinaigrette: In a small bowl, whisk together the lemon juice, vinegar, mustard, and sugar. Gradually whisk in the olive oil until emulsified. Season with salt and pepper to taste.

Transfer the green beans to a serving bowl. Add the onion and vinaigrette. Toss to coat evenly. Season with salt and pepper to taste. Divide among small plates. Sprinkle each with an equal amount of the blue cheese and almonds and serve.

Note: To toast nuts, preheat the oven to 350°F. Spread the nuts on a sided baking sheet and bake until aromatic, following the time chart below for each type of nut. Be careful not to burn the nuts, as most have a high oil content that makes them toast quickly and burn easily.

Almonds: 7 to 10 minutes for whole, about 5 minutes for sliced
Pecans: 5 to 7 minutes
Pine nuts: 5 to 7 minutes
Walnuts: 7 to 10 minutes

Serves 6

1½ pounds green beans, trimmed

Vinaigrette
1 tablespoon freshly squeezed lemon juice
1 tablespoon white wine vinegar
1 teaspoon Dijon mustard
½ teaspoon sugar
¼ cup olive oil
Kosher salt and freshly ground white pepper

½ red onion, thinly sliced
Kosher salt and freshly ground black pepper
½ cup (2 ounces) crumbled blue cheese
⅓ cup sliced almonds, toasted (see Note)

Wine pairing: Riesling

mediterranean cucumber salad

Serves 6

Vinaigrette

1 tablespoon red wine vinegar

1 tablespoon freshly squeezed lemon juice

1½ teaspoons honey

1½ teaspoons chopped fresh chives

¼ teaspoon kosher salt

⅛ teaspoon freshly ground white pepper

Pinch of dried thyme

3 tablespoons canola oil

1 tablespoon olive oil

1 large English cucumber (about 1¼ pounds),

   peeled and cut into thin diagonal slices

1 carrot, peeled, halved lengthwise, and cut into

   thin diagonal slices

1 green onion (white and green parts), cut into

   thin diagonal slices

8 kalamata olives, pitted and halved lengthwise

1 teaspoon capers, drained

½ cup (2½ ounces) crumbled goat cheese

Wine pairing: Sauvignon Blanc

For the vinaigrette: In a small bowl, whisk together the vinegar, lemon juice, honey, chives, salt, pepper, and thyme. Gradually whisk in the canola and olive oils in a slow, steady stream until emulsified.

In a large bowl, combine the cucumber, carrot, green onion, olives, and capers. Add the vinaigrette and toss to coat evenly. Let stand for 15 minutes to let the flavors meld. Divide among 6 small bowls, top each with an equal amount of goat cheese, and serve.

greek bread salad

Serves 6

5 cups (about 4 ounces) cubed stale country bread

    such as levain

⅓ cup extra-virgin olive oil

2 tablespoons freshly squeezed lemon juice

12 ounces colorful heirloom tomatoes, seeded and

    coarsely chopped

1 small cucumber (6 ounces), peeled, seeded, and

    cut into ½-inch dice

¾ cup (4 ounces) crumbled feta cheese

⅓ cup pitted green olives, chopped

⅓ cup diced red onion

2 tablespoons capers, drained and rinsed

2 tablespoons minced fresh lemon or regular thyme

2 tablespoons minced fresh flat-leaf parsley

1 tablespoon minced fresh chives

1 tablespoon minced fresh basil

2 teaspoons minced fresh oregano

Kosher salt and freshly ground black pepper

Wine pairing: Sauvignon Blanc

Put the bread in a large bowl. In a small bowl, whisk the olive oil and lemon juice together. Pour over the bread and toss to coat well. Stir in all the remaining ingredients, reserving a small portion of the feta and herbs to use as garnish. Let stand for 30 minutes to let the flavors meld. Divide among 6 small bowls and garnish with the reserved feta and herbs.

peach salad with arugula, bacon, and mint

Serves 6

In a small skillet, fry the bacon, stirring often, over medium-low heat until crisp, 8 to 10 minutes. Using a slotted spoon, transfer to paper towels to drain.

In a blender, combine half of one peach and the lemon juice. Puree until smooth. With the machine running, gradually add the canola and olive oils in a slow, steady stream. Add the shallots and pulse to blend. Season with salt to taste.

Put the arugula in a large bowl and add three-fourths of the vinaigrette. Toss to coat evenly. Divide among 6 small plates. Put the peaches in the bowl and add the remaining vinaigrette. Toss to coat evenly. Arrange an equal amount of peaches on top of each bed of arugula. Sprinkle each serving with a pinch of salt. Top each with an equal amount of bacon and mint. Serve.

2 to 3 thick slices bacon, diced

1 pound (about 3) ripe peaches, peeled, pitted, and sliced

2 tablespoons freshly squeezed lemon juice

3 tablespoons canola oil

1 tablespoon extra-virgin olive oil

2 tablespoons minced shallots

Kosher salt

5 ounces (about 6 loosely packed cups) arugula

2 tablespoons fresh mint, chopped in a fine chiffonade

Wine pairing: Riesling

caramelized pear and walnut salad with prosciutto

Serves 6

Vinaigrette

1 cup freshly squeezed orange juice

2 teaspoons red wine vinegar

1 teaspoon dry white wine

1 tablespoon chopped red onion

1 teaspoon sugar

¼ cup extra-virgin olive oil

1 tablespoon unsalted butter

2 Bosc pears, peeled, cored, and cut into ½-inch-thick wedges

¾ cup walnut halves

¼ cup sugar

¼ cup water

2 romaine lettuce hearts, torn into bite-sized pieces

2 ounces thinly sliced prosciutto, cut into thin strips

Wine pairing: Chardonnay

For the vinaigrette: In a small saucepan, bring the orange juice to a boil over medium-high heat. Cook, stirring often, until reduced to about ⅓ cup, 7 to 10 minutes. Pour into a blender. Add the vinegar, wine, onion, and sugar and puree. With the machine running, gradually add the oil in a slow, steady stream. Refrigerate until chilled, about 15 minutes.

In a medium skillet, melt the butter over medium heat. Add the pears and walnuts. Cook for 3 minutes, stirring occasionally. Stir in the ¼ cup sugar and the water and bring to a boil. Cook, stirring often, until the sugar begins to brown, about 10 minutes. Remove from the heat and let cool.

Put the lettuce in a large bowl. Add half of the vinaigrette and toss to coat evenly. Arrange the lettuce on 6 serving plates. Top each with an equal amount of the prosciutto and the pear mixture. Drizzle the remaining vinaigrette over the top and serve.

romaine, apple, and cranberry salad

Serves 6

In a large bowl, combine the apples, sliced romaine hearts, and cranberries.

In a small bowl, stir together the mayonnaise, vinegar, and chives. Pour over the apple mixture and stir gently to coat. Season with salt to taste. Arrange the whole lettuce leaves on a large platter or divide among 6 salad plates. Arrange an equal amount of the apple mixture on top of each lettuce leaf and top each with an equal amount of the pecans.

2 sweet-tart apples, such as Pink Lady or Gravenstein, peeled, cored, and cut into fine julienne

4 cups (4 ounces) thinly sliced romaine lettuce hearts, plus 6 whole larger heart leaves

½ cup dried cranberries, chopped

¼ cup mayonnaise

2 tablespoons apple cider vinegar

2 tablespoons minced fresh chives

Kosher salt

¼ cup pecans, toasted (see page 21) and chopped

Wine pairing: Chardonnay

vegetables

asparagus bundles with melted brie

Serves 6

Preheat the oven to 350°F. In a large pot of salted boiling water, cook the asparagus until crisp-tender, 2 to 3 minutes. Using tongs, transfer to a colander to drain.

Add the green onion leaves to the boiling water and cook for 30 seconds. Drain in a colander and rinse under cold running water to stop the cooking.

In a small skillet, melt the butter over medium heat. Add the bread crumbs and sesame seeds and sauté until browned, about 2 minutes.

Arrange the asparagus in 6 bundles of 3 spears each and tie each bundle together with a green onion leaf. Arrange the asparagus bundles in a shallow baking pan. Place 1 slice of Brie on top of each bundle. Sprinkle each bundle equally with the bread crumb mixture. Bake until the cheese melts, 6 to 8 minutes. Sprinkle with salt and pepper and serve each bundle on a small plate.

18 spears asparagus, trimmed

Green leaves (about 6 inches long) of 6 green onions

1 tablespoon unsalted butter

¼ cup dried bread crumbs

2 tablespoons sesame seeds

6 thin slices (about 3 ounces total) Brie cheese

Kosher salt and freshly ground black pepper

Wine pairing: Sauvignon Blanc or Riesling

spring vegetable ragout with pepper-parmesan crostini

Serves 6

Pepper-Parmesan Crostini

Twelve ¼-inch-thick diagonal baguette slices

1 tablespoon olive oil for brushing

¼ cup grated Parmesan cheese

Freshly cracked black pepper

1 pound fresh fava beans, shelled, or 1 cup frozen shelled soybeans

3 tablespoons unsalted butter

1 tablespoon olive oil

1 leek (white and light green parts only), rinsed and thinly sliced

1 teaspoon minced garlic

2½ cups rich vegetable broth

1 cup baby carrots, quartered lengthwise

2 cups thinly sliced Swiss chard leaves

8 ounces asparagus, cut into 1-inch diagonal slices

½ cup minced mixed fresh herbs, such as basil, parsley, tarragon, chervil, and chives

4 ounces fresh sugar snap peas, halved crosswise

Kosher salt and freshly ground black pepper

Wine pairing: Chardonnay

For the crostini: Preheat the oven to 350°F. Brush each slice of bread with a little olive oil on one side. Arrange on a baking sheet and top each with equal amounts of Parmesan. Sprinkle with a little pepper and bake until crisp, 8 to 10 minutes.

In a large pot of salted boiling water, blanch the fava beans for 1 minute. Drain in a colander and rinse under cold water to stop the cooking. Peel the skins from the beans and discard the skins.

In a large skillet, melt 1 tablespoon of the butter with the olive oil over medium heat. Add the leek and sauté until translucent, about 4 minutes. Add the garlic and sauté until fragrant, 1 minute. Stir in the broth and carrots and cook until the carrots are crisp-tender, about 8 minutes. Stir in the chard and cook until wilted, about 3 minutes. (If using soybeans, add them now.) Add the asparagus, cover, and cook until crisp-tender, about 4 minutes. Stir in the herbs, sugar snap peas, and fava beans.

Add the remaining 2 tablespoons butter, 1 tablespoon at a time, stirring gently. Season with salt and pepper to taste. Divide among 6 individual bowls and top each with 2 crostini.

grilled eggplant and tomatoes

Serves 6

Line a baking sheet with paper towels. Put the eggplant slices on the prepared pan and sprinkle with salt. Let stand for about 20 minutes to extract any excess moisture. Pat dry using a paper towel.

Preheat a gas grill to medium-high. Brush the eggplant and tomato slices using the ¼ cup olive oil. Sprinkle generously with the oregano and pepper. Sprinkle the tomato slices with salt.

Place the eggplant slices on the grill and cook until tender and nicely browned, about 5 minutes per side. Transfer to a plate. Put the tomato slices on the grill and cook until grill marks appear, about 1 minute per side. Transfer to a plate.

In a small bowl, stir together the remaining 1 tablespoon olive oil, the vinegar, capers, and orange zest. Season with salt and pepper to taste.

To serve, arrange an equal number of eggplant and tomato slices on each of 6 small plates. Drizzle the vinaigrette over each serving and sprinkle with the basil. Serve.

1 pound Japanese eggplants, cut into ½-inch-thick lengthwise slices

Sea salt

1½ pounds small, firm tomatoes, cut into ½-inch-thick slices

¼ cup olive oil, plus 1 tablespoon

1 teaspoon dried oregano

Freshly ground black pepper

1 tablespoon balsamic vinegar

1 teaspoon capers, drained and chopped

½ teaspoon grated orange zest

¼ cup fresh basil leaves, torn into small pieces

Wine pairing: Pinot Noir or Merlot

chilled corn soup
with meyer lemon olive oil

Serves 6

6 ears corn, shucked

3 cups milk

1 cup heavy cream

Kosher salt and freshly ground black pepper

Meyer lemon olive oil for garnish (see Note)

1 tablespoon minced fresh chives

Wine pairing: Chardonnay or Rosé

Cut the corn kernels from the cobs and set aside. Put the cobs in a large stockpot and add the milk. Bring to a boil over medium heat. Reduce the heat to low and simmer until reduced by two-thirds, about 20 minutes. Add the corn kernels and cream and simmer until the kernels are tender, about 5 minutes. Remove the cobs and discard.

In batches, transfer the corn mixture to a blender and puree. Strain through a fine-meshed sieve into a bowl and season with salt and pepper to taste. Refrigerate until chilled, 4 to 6 hours.

Divide among 6 small bowls and drizzle a liberal amount of Meyer lemon olive oil over each serving. Sprinkle with chives and serve.

Note: Olive oil flavored with Meyer lemons is readily available in specialty foods stores and can often be found next to other olive oils in supermarkets.

ratatouille with summer herbs

Serves 6

Preheat the oven to 400°F. Put the eggplant in a colander and sprinkle with the salt. Let stand until moisture begins to bead on the surface of the eggplant, about 15 minutes.

Pat the eggplant dry. Spread on a sided baking sheet and pour ¼ cup of the olive oil over the eggplant. Toss to coat evenly. Sprinkle with the 1 teaspoon salt. Bake, turning once or twice, until tender, 25 to 30 minutes.

In a large skillet, heat the remaining ¼ cup olive oil over medium-high heat. Add the onion and sauté until browned, 5 to 7 minutes. Add the zucchini, bell pepper, and garlic. Reduce the heat to medium and sauté until the pepper is tender, about 10 minutes. Stir in the tomatoes and tomato paste. Cook, stirring often, until the tomatoes have melted, about 20 minutes. Add the eggplant and cook until the flavors meld, about 10 minutes. Stir in the basil, sage, and oregano. Season with pepper and adjust the seasonings to taste. Divide among 6 small plates and serve.

1 globe eggplant (about 1 pound), unpeeled and cut into 1-inch cubes

Kosher salt for sprinkling, plus 1 teaspoon

½ cup olive oil

1 sweet onion, cut into 1-inch cubes

2 zucchini, cut into 1-inch cubes

½ red bell pepper, seeded and cut into 1-inch squares

1 tablespoon minced garlic

1 pound ripe tomatoes, seeded and chopped

⅓ cup tomato paste

3 tablespoons minced fresh basil

1 tablespoon minced fresh sage

1 tablespoon minced fresh oregano

Freshly ground black pepper

Wine pairing: Zinfandel or Syrah

grilled eggplant–red pepper rolls

Serves 6

⅓ cup extra-virgin olive oil, plus oil for brushing and more

    if needed for puree

2 cloves garlic, lightly crushed and peeled

3 unpeeled large Japanese eggplants

2 red bell peppers

Kosher salt

¼ cup grated Parmesan cheese

2 tablespoons chopped oil-packed sun-dried tomatoes

1 tablespoon pine nuts

1½ cups loosely packed fresh basil leaves

Wine pairing: Merlot, Cabernet Sauvignon, or Meritage

In a small skillet, combine the ⅓ cup olive oil and the garlic. Cook over low heat until the garlic is aromatic, about 15 minutes. Be careful not to burn the garlic. Remove from the heat.

Meanwhile, cut the eggplants in half lengthwise. Cut 3 or 4 slices (each about ⅛ inch thick) from each eggplant half with a mandoline or a very sharp knife, starting on the cut side of each half. You should have at least 18 slices; prepare a few extra in case some tear in grilling or rolling. Cut the red peppers into quarters lengthwise; seed, devein, and brush lightly with olive oil.

Preheat a gas grill to medium. Place the pepper quarters on the grill and close the lid. Grill, turning occasionally, until the skin is blistered and blackened and the flesh is tender, 12 to 15 minutes. Place in a resealable plastic bag, seal, and let stand until cool to the touch, about 15 minutes. Peel and cut into ¼-inch-thick strips. Increase the grill heat to medium-high and brush the eggplant slices lightly with the garlic oil. Season with salt to taste. Grill the eggplant until grill-marked and tender, about 1 minute per side. Stack on a plate and cover loosely with plastic wrap.

In a blender, combine the cheese, sun-dried tomatoes, pine nuts, half of the basil, and the remaining garlic oil. Puree until smooth, adding more olive oil if needed to make the blending easier.

One at a time, place the eggplant slices on a work surface. Spread lightly with the basil mixture and top with a leaf or two of the remaining basil leaves and a few strips of roasted pepper. Carefully roll up and place, seam side down, on a platter or arrange 3 rolls on each of 6 small plates and serve.

golden chanterelle–topped crostini

Serves 6

Preheat the oven to 350°F. Brush the baguette slices with 2 tablespoons of the olive oil. Arrange on a baking sheet and bake until crisp, 7 to 10 minutes.

In a large skillet, heat the remaining 1 tablespoon olive oil over medium heat. Add the mushrooms and sauté until browned, about 3 minutes. Add the wine and sauté until almost dry, about 3 minutes. Stir in the butter, shallots, and thyme and sauté until butter is browned and shallots are translucent, about 3 minutes. Season with salt and pepper to taste.

Spread each crostini with 1 teaspoon of the fromage blanc or ricotta and top with an equal amount of the mushroom mixture. Arrange 3 crostini on each of 6 small plates and serve.

Eighteen ¼-inch-thick diagonal baguette slices

3 tablespoons olive oil

4 ounces chanterelle mushrooms, cleaned and sliced into ¼-inch thick strips

¼ cup dry white wine

2 tablespoons unsalted butter

2 tablespoons minced shallots

½ teaspoon minced fresh thyme

Kosher salt and freshly ground black pepper

⅓ cup fromage blanc or fresh ricotta cheese

Wine pairing: Pinot Noir

fennel and gorgonzola gratin

Serves 6

3 small fennel bulbs (about 2 pounds total), trimmed

    and halved lengthwise (fennel fronds reserved)

1 cup chicken stock or low-sodium broth

½ cup (about 2 ounces) crumbled Gorgonzola cheese

1 tablespoon dried bread crumbs

Wine pairing: Chardonnay

Mince enough of the fennel fronds to yield 1 tablespoon. Put the fennel halves, cut side down, in a skillet large enough to hold the fennel in a single layer. Add the stock and bring to a boil over high heat. Reduce the heat to low, cover, and simmer until the fennel is tender, 15 to 20 minutes. Using a slotted spoon, transfer the fennel halves and place, cut side up, in 6 small gratin dishes.

Return the stock to high heat and boil until reduced to ⅓ cup, 2 to 3 minutes. Stir in the minced fennel fronds. Pour over the fennel halves.

Preheat the oven to 375°F. In a small bowl, mash the Gorgonzola with a fork. Stir in the bread crumbs and spoon an equal amount over each fennel half. Bake until the cheese is melted, about 10 minutes. Serve hot.

balsamic-glazed potatoes and onions

Serves 6

In a large pot of salted boiling water, blanch the onions for 1 to 2 minutes. Drain in a colander and rinse with cold water. When cool to the touch, peel the onions by trimming away the root end from each onion and slipping off the skin.

Preheat the oven to 350°F. Peel a ½-inch strip around the center of each potato. Put the potatoes and onions in a baking dish large enough to hold them in a single layer. In a small bowl, combine the vinegar and butter and pour over the potatoes. Sprinkle generously with salt and pepper and toss to coat evenly. Nestle the 2 rosemary sprigs and 2 sage sprigs among the potatoes and cover with a lid or aluminum foil. Bake, turning every 20 minutes, until the potatoes are tender, about 1 hour.

To serve, divide among 6 small bowls or plates, garnish each with a rosemary sprig or sage leaf, and serve.

1 pound pearl onions

1 pound small (about 1 inch in diameter) Yukon Gold potatoes, unpeeled and scrubbed

2 tablespoons balsamic vinegar

1 tablespoon unsalted butter, melted

Kosher salt and freshly ground black pepper

2 rosemary sprigs, plus more for garnish

2 sage leaves, plus more for garnish

Wine pairing: Merlot or Syrah

roasted brussels sprouts
with chorizo

Serves 6

2 tablespoons raisins

1¼ pounds Brussels sprouts, quartered

3 tablespoons olive oil

4 ounces Spanish chorizo, cut into small pieces

1 tablespoon unsalted butter

2 tablespoons minced shallots

1 teaspoon minced fresh thyme

2 tablespoons sherry vinegar

Kosher salt and freshly ground black pepper

Wine pairing: Pinot Noir or Syrah

Preheat the oven to 400°F. Put the raisins in a small bowl and add hot water to cover. Let stand until plumped, about 10 minutes. Drain.

Put the Brussels sprouts in a large roasting pan in a single layer. Drizzle with the olive oil. Bake, stirring occasionally, until browned and tender, about 25 minutes. Stir in the chorizo, butter, shallots, and thyme and return to the oven until the chorizo is sizzling, about 5 minutes longer.

Stir in the raisins, vinegar, salt, and pepper. Divide among 6 small plates and serve.

grilled celery with truffle oil

Serves 6

Preheat a gas grill to high.

Peel the fibrous outer layer from the celery stalks with a vegetable peeler. Cut each stalk into three 4-inch lengths. Put the celery in a large bowl and add the olive oil and a pinch of salt. Toss to coat evenly. Place on the grill, cover, and cook until slightly tender and grill-marked, 2 to 3 minutes per side.

Transfer the celery to 6 small plates and arrange in a stack on each. Sprinkle with pine nuts and a little salt. Drizzle with the truffle oil and vinegar. Shave an equal amount of the cheese over each portion. Serve.

10 large celery stalks, each 12 inches long

2 tablespoons olive oil

Kosher salt

2 tablespoons pine nuts, toasted (see page 21)

About 1 teaspoon black truffle oil

1 tablespoon balsamic vinegar

1 small chunk Parmigiano-Reggiano cheese

Wine pairing: Chardonnay or Pinot Noir

roasted cauliflower with braised radicchio

Serves 6

1½ pounds small cauliflower florets, halved or quartered

    if larger than 1 inch

4 tablespoons olive oil

1 tablespoon unsalted butter

1 clove garlic, minced

½ teaspoon red pepper flakes

One 15-ounce can kidney beans, drained

1 tablespoon minced fresh flat-leaf parsley

1 tablespoon chopped fresh chives

Kosher salt and freshly ground black pepper

1 head radicchio, cut into 6 wedges

¼ cup balsamic vinegar

Wine pairing: Zinfandel

Preheat the oven to 400°F. Put the cauliflower florets in a single layer in a large roasting pan and drizzle with 3 tablespoons of the olive oil. Bake, stirring occasionally, until browned and tender, 25 to 30 minutes. Remove from the oven and stir in the butter, garlic, and red pepper flakes. Return to the oven and roast until the garlic is fragrant, about 5 minutes. Stir in the kidney beans, parsley, and chives. Season with salt and pepper. Set aside.

In a medium-size heavy skillet, heat the remaining 1 tablespoon olive oil over high heat. Add the radicchio and sauté until evenly browned, 2 to 3 minutes per side. Add the vinegar and cook until reduced and thick, about 5 minutes, turning the radicchio several times.

Place a radicchio wedge on each of 6 small plates. Spoon an equal amount of the cauliflower mixture over or next to each wedge and serve.

seafood

molasses-almond shrimp on spicy cabbage salad

Serves 6

6 cups shredded napa cabbage

1 small carrot, julienned

½ red bell pepper, seeded, deveined, and julienned

½ small seedless cucumber, peeled, seeded, and julienned

4 ounces julienned jicama

3 green onions (white and green parts), cut into thin diagonal slices

¼ cup *each,* loosely packed fresh mint, basil,

　　flat-leaf parsley, and cilantro, coarsely chopped

3 tablespoons sesame oil

3 tablespoons freshly squeezed lime juice

2 tablespoons seasoned rice vinegar

2 tablespoons tamari soy sauce

1 teaspoon sugar

1 teaspoon minced seeded serrano chile

½ teaspoon grated fresh ginger

3 tablespoons peanut oil

Kosher salt and freshly ground black pepper

1 cup almonds, toasted (see page 21) and finely chopped

1 tablespoon olive oil

18 large shrimp, shelled and deveined, with tails left on

2 tablespoons light molasses

Sliced almonds, for garnish

Wine pairing: Muscat Canelli or Riesling

In a large bowl, combine the cabbage, carrot, bell pepper, cucumber, jicama, green onions, and fresh herbs.

In a small bowl, whisk together the sesame oil, lime juice, vinegar, tamari, sugar, chile, and ginger until the sugar dissolves. Gradually whisk in the peanut oil in a slow, steady stream. Pour over the cabbage mixture and refrigerate about 15 minutes. Season with salt and pepper to taste.

Put the chopped almonds in a shallow bowl. In a large skillet, heat the olive oil over medium-high heat. Add the shrimp and sauté, turning as needed, until evenly pink, 2 to 3 minutes. Remove from the heat. Add the molasses to the pan and toss to coat the shrimp evenly. Roll the shrimp in the almonds to coat evenly.

Divide the cabbage mixture among 6 small plates. Top each serving with 3 shrimp and garnish with sliced almonds. Serve at once.

curry-dusted halibut
with arugula and jasmine rice

Serves 6

In a fine-meshed sieve, rinse the rice thoroughly in cold water. In a medium saucepan, combine the rice and 1½ cups water. Bring to a boil over high heat, reduce to low, cover, and cook until the rice is tender, about 15 minutes. Remove from heat and let stand 5 minutes. Fluff with a fork before serving.

In a medium bowl, combine the arugula, lemon juice, and olive oil. Toss to coat evenly. Season with salt and pepper to taste. Divide among 6 small plates.

In a small bowl, mix together the curry powder, the remaining ½ teaspoon salt, and the cayenne. Rub the curry mixture over both sides of the halibut pieces. In a large skillet, heat the canola oil over high heat until it shimmers but is not smoking. Add the halibut and cook until browned, 2 to 3 minutes per side. Using tongs, place a piece of halibut on top of each arugula bed and arrange a mound of rice next to it. Serve.

1 cup jasmine rice

1½ cups water

3 cups loosely packed arugula leaves

1 tablespoon freshly squeezed lemon juice

1 tablespoon extra-virgin olive oil

Kosher salt, plus ½ teaspoon

Freshly ground black pepper

1 teaspoon curry powder

Pinch of cayenne pepper

Three 4- to 6-ounce halibut fillets, each cut in half

1 tablespoon canola oil

Wine pairing: Rosé or Riesling

prawn skewers
with lime marinade

Serves 6

24 large tiger prawns, shelled and deveined,

    with tails left on

½ cup chopped white onion

1 teaspoon grated lime zest

2 tablespoons freshly squeezed lime juice

1 tablespoon canola oil

1 tablespoon minced fresh ginger

1 to 2 teaspoons minced jalapeño chile

1 clove garlic, minced

Lime wedges, for serving

Wine pairing: Riesling or Rosé

Rinse the prawns, pat dry, and place in a resealable plastic bag.

In a blender, combine the onion, lime zest, lime juice, oil, ginger, jalapeño, and garlic and puree until smooth. (If too thick, add a bit more oil.) Adjust the jalapeño to your taste. Pour over the prawns, turn the bag to coat, seal, and refrigerate for 4 hours.

Preheat a gas grill to medium-high. Soak twelve 6-inch bamboo skewers in water for 20 minutes. Remove the prawns from the refrigerator.

Thread 2 prawns through both ends onto each skewer. Discard the marinade.

Brush the grill grids with oil and place the prawns on the grill. Cook until the prawns are evenly pink, 1½ to 2 minutes per side. Remove from the grill, divide among 6 small plates, and serve warm with lime wedges.

seared tuna with hazelnuts and pink peppercorns on couscous

Serves 6

Preheat the oven to 350°F. Put the hazelnuts on a sided baking sheet and bake until lightly toasted and fragrant, about 10 minutes. Wrap the hazelnuts in a kitchen towel and rub them together to remove the skins. Finely chop the hazelnuts and put in a small bowl.

Put the peppercorns in a sealable plastic bag and crush with a rolling pin or mallet. In a small bowl, combine the crushed pepper, lemon zest, and salt; mix well. Rub half of the mixture over both sides of the tuna; stir the remaining half into the hazelnuts and set aside.

For the couscous: In a medium saucepan, bring the water, butter, and salt to a boil. Remove from the heat, add the couscous, and cover. Let stand for 5 minutes. Fluff with a fork and stir in the cilantro and lemon juice. Arrange in a mound on each of 6 small plates.

In a medium nonstick skillet, heat the oil over high heat until it shimmers but is not yet smoking. Add the tuna and cook 1 to 2 minutes. Turn and sear the other side, about 1 minute. (It will be rare on the inside.) Transfer the tuna to a cutting board and cut into thin slices. Fan a few slices over each mound of couscous, sprinkle equally with the hazelnut mixture, and serve with lemon wedges.

¼ cup hazelnuts

2 tablespoons pink peppercorns

2 teaspoons grated lemon zest

1 teaspoon kosher salt

One 12-ounce piece sushi-grade ahi tuna, at least 1 inch thick

Couscous

1¼ cups water

1 tablespoon unsalted butter

¼ teaspoon salt

1 cup couscous

2 tablespoons chopped fresh cilantro

1 tablespoon freshly squeezed lemon juice

1 teaspoon canola oil

Lemon wedges, for serving

Wine pairing: Chardonnay

crab salad with rémoulade

Serves 6

Rémoulade Sauce

½ cup mayonnaise

1½ tablespoons freshly squeezed lemon juice

1 tablespoon ketchup

1 teaspoon Creole or stone-ground mustard

1 teaspoon Spanish smoked sweet paprika (pimentón dulce)

¼ teaspoon curry powder

¼ cup finely diced celery

1 tablespoon minced shallot

2 teaspoons minced fresh chives

Kosher salt and freshly ground black pepper

2 cups cauliflower florets, cut in half if larger than 1 inch

4 cups thinly sliced napa cabbage

1 tablespoon olive oil

1 tablespoon rice wine vinegar

12 ounces fresh lump crabmeat, picked over for shell

2 tablespoons minced fresh chives

Wine pairing: Chardonnay or Rosé

In a small bowl, whisk together the mayonnaise, lemon juice, ketchup, and mustard. Stir in the paprika and curry powder. Fold in the celery, shallot, and chives. Season with salt and pepper to taste. Cover and refrigerate until ready to use.

In a large pot of salted boiling water, cook the cauliflower until crisp-tender, about 2 minutes. Drain in a colander and rinse under cold water to stop the cooking. Let cool.

In a medium bowl, toss the cabbage with the olive oil and vinegar. Divide among 6 small plates or shallow bowls.

Put the cauliflower in the bowl that held the cabbage. Stir in the crabmeat and rémoulade. Spoon equal amounts of the mixture over the cabbage and sprinkle with the 2 tablespoons chives. Serve.

paprika-spiced grilled calamari with cannellini beans

Serves 6

In a medium bowl, combine the olive oil, garlic, paprika, and lemon zest. Stir to blend. Add the calamari and toss to coat evenly. Let stand for 1 hour.

Soak 8 large bamboo skewers in water for 20 minutes if you don't have a grill basket.

For the vinaigrette: In a small bowl, whisk together the vinegar, lemon juice, Worcestershire, shallot, and garlic. Let stand for 5 to 10 minutes. Gradually whisk in the oil in a slow, steady stream.

In a large bowl, combine the beans and parsley. Add the vinaigrette and toss to coat evenly. Season with salt and pepper to taste. Divide among 6 shallow bowls or small plates.

Preheat a gas grill to high. Thread the calamari pieces onto the skewers or place in a single layer in an oiled grill basket. Place the calamari on the grill, and cook, covered, until opaque, 1 to 2 minutes per side. (Be careful not to overcook.) Transfer to a cutting board and cut into 1-inch pieces. Arrange equal amounts of calamari over each serving of beans, season with salt and pepper, and serve immediately, with lemon wedges.

2 tablespoons olive oil

2 cloves garlic, minced

2 teaspoons Spanish smoked sweet paprika (pimentón dulce)

1 teaspoon grated lemon zest

12 ounces cleaned calamari, including tentacles

Vinaigrette

1 tablespoon rice wine vinegar

1 tablespoon freshly squeezed lemon juice

½ teaspoon Worcestershire sauce

1 tablespoon minced shallot

1 small clove garlic, minced

2 tablespoons extra-virgin olive oil

Two (15-ounce) cans cannellini or white beans, drained and rinsed

¼ cup fresh flat-leaf parsley leaves

Kosher salt and freshly ground black pepper

Lemon wedges, for serving

Wine pairing: Riesling or Pinot Noir

scallops on blood orange and watercress salad

Serves 6

3 blood oranges

1 tablespoon Champagne vinegar

2 tablespoons minced shallots

3 tablespoons extra-virgin olive oil

12 ounces watercress, stemmed

Sea salt and freshly ground black pepper

6 large (2-ounce) diver or day-boat sea scallops, sliced in half,

    or 12 medium (1-ounce) scallops, patted dry

Wine pairing: Sauvignon Blanc

Cut the skin from two of the oranges, following the curve of the fruit with the knife. Carefully cut the sections from the membranes, working over a small bowl to catch any juice. Put the segments in a large bowl.

Measure 2 tablespoons of the juice and transfer to a small bowl. (If there is less than 2 tablespoons, squeeze enough from the remaining orange to yield 2 tablespoons.) Whisk in the vinegar and shallots. Gradually whisk in 2 tablespoons of the olive oil in a slow, steady stream. Add to the bowl with the orange segments. Add the watercress and toss gently to coat evenly. Season with salt and pepper to taste. Divide among 6 small plates.

Season the scallops with salt and pepper. In a large sauté pan, heat the remaining 1 tablespoon olive oil over high heat until it shimmers but does not smoke. Add the scallops and cook until browned on the bottom, about 2 minutes (slightly less for smaller scallops). Turn and cook until other side is browned, 1 to 2 minutes. Divide the scallops among the plates of salad and serve immediately.

capellini with clams

Serves 6

In a large, heavy saucepan, melt the butter over medium-high heat and cook until the butter is brown and has released a nutty aroma, 3 to 4 minutes. Add the clams, increase the heat to high, and stir in the wine. Cover and cook until the clams open, 4 to 6 minutes. Transfer the clams with tongs or a slotted spoon to a plate. Discard any clams that don't open.

Meanwhile, in a large pot of salted boiling water, cook the pasta until al dente, about 6 to 8 minutes. Drain the pasta and add to the pan with the butter mixture. Add the parsley and chives. Season with salt and pepper to taste. Toss to coat evenly. Divide the pasta among 6 small plates, top each serving with an equal number of clams, and serve.

6 tablespoons unsalted butter

1½ pounds clams, scrubbed

½ cup dry white wine

12 ounces capellini or angel hair pasta

½ cup loosely packed fresh flat-leaf parsley, coarsely chopped

1 bunch chives, cut into ½-inch pieces

Kosher salt and freshly ground black pepper

Wine pairing: Chardonnay

citrus-cured salmon on blini

Serves 6

One 1-pound salmon fillet

¼ cup kosher salt

2 tablespoons sugar

2 teaspoons fennel seeds, lightly crushed

1 teaspoon grated lemon zest

1 teaspoon grated lime zest

Blini

½ cup lukewarm milk, about 105°F

1 large egg, separated

2 tablespoons sour cream or crème fraîche, plus ¼ cup

1 tablespoon unsalted butter, melted, plus 1 teaspoon for frying

2 teaspoons (1 envelope) rapid-rise yeast

1 cup all-purpose flour

½ teaspoon salt

½ teaspoon sugar

1 teaspoon canola oil

1 tablespoon minced fresh chives

Wine pairing: Sauvignon Blanc

Lay the salmon on a work surface and run your hand over the meat side to find the pin bones. Remove the bones with fish tweezers or needle-nose pliers.

In a small bowl, combine the salt, sugar, fennel seeds, lemon zest, and lime zest. Stir to blend. Rub over the meat side of the salmon to form a thin, even coating covering all of the meat. Wrap tightly in plastic wrap, place in a baking pan, and place a heavy pan on top to weight the fish down. Refrigerate for 24 hours.

(continued on next page)

For the blini: In a small bowl, combine the milk, egg yolk, the 2 tablespoons sour cream or crème fraîche, and the melted butter. Whisk to blend. Stir in the yeast until dissolved and let stand about 10 minutes.

In a medium bowl, combine the flour, salt, and sugar. Stir with a whisk to blend. Stir in the milk mixture until just blended. Cover the bowl with plastic wrap and let stand until well risen (about double in size), about 2 hours at room temperature or up to 8 hours in the refrigerator.

Remove the salmon from the refrigerator, unwrap, and wipe off the salt mixture. Place the salmon on a work surface, skin side up. Using a very sharp knife, cut away the skin by guiding the blade of the knife along the skin with one hand while cutting with the other. Cut the salmon into paper-thin slices.

In a medium bowl, beat the egg white until stiff peaks form. Fold into the batter.

Preheat the oven to 200°F. Heat a nonstick griddle or a large skillet over medium-high heat. Add half of the 1 teaspoon butter and ½ teaspoon of the oil; when the butter sizzles, wipe pan with a wadded paper towel. Using a tablespoon, spoon 6 equal-size dollops of the batter into the pan spaced a few inches apart. Cook until bubbles appear on the surface and browned on the bottom, about 2 minutes. Turn and cook until well browned on the second side, 1 to 2 minutes more. Transfer to a plate in the oven to keep warm; repeat to cook 6 more blini.

Arrange a slice of salmon on top of each blini (reserve any remaining salmon for other uses). Top each with a dollop of the ¼ cup sour cream or crème fraîche and a tiny bit of chives. Place 2 blini on each of 6 small plates and serve.

meat & poultry

Using a vegetable peeler, peel twelve ½-inch-wide strips of zest from the top to the bottom of 2 of the lemons and set aside. (If using a mixture of oranges and lemons, peel zest from the orange.) Juice all 3 lemons (or the orange and lemon) into a measuring cup; you should have ½ cup.

In a large bowl, combine ¼ cup of the juice, the 2 tablespoons olive oil, 1 teaspoon of the garlic, the oregano, and bay leaves. Add the chicken, lemon strips, and onions and toss to coat evenly. Cover and refrigerate for at least 2 hours or up to 4 hours.

Soak twelve 8-inch bamboo skewers in water for 20 minutes.

In a food processor, combine the remaining ¼ cup juice, remaining 1 teaspoon garlic, the green onions, basil, cilantro, parsley, tarragon, orange zest, cayenne, allspice, cumin, and cinnamon. Process until smooth. With the machine running, gradually add the remaining ½ cup olive oil in a slow, steady stream until thoroughly incorporated.

Preheat a gas grill to medium-high. Thread the chicken on the skewers, alternating with the lemon strips, bay leaves, and onion pieces. Brush lightly with olive oil. Sprinkle with salt and pepper. Place in the center of the grill, cover, and cook, turning once or twice, until opaque throughout, 5 to 8 minutes. Divide among 6 small plates. Serve the sauce in small bowls alongside.

lemon-chicken kebabs with moroccan herb sauce

Serves 6

3 Meyer lemons, or 1 large orange and 1 regular lemon

2 tablespoons extra-virgin olive oil, plus ½ cup,

plus oil for brushing

2 teaspoons minced garlic

½ teaspoon dried oregano

12 fresh bay leaves (omit if not available)

1 large skinless, boneless whole chicken breast

(about 1 pound), cut into 1-inch cubes

2 large sweet onions, each cut into 12 wedges

2 green onions (white and green parts), coarsely chopped

2 tablespoons *each* chopped fresh basil, cilantro,

and flat-leaf parsley

1 teaspoon chopped fresh tarragon

1 teaspoon grated orange zest

1 pinch *each* cayenne pepper, allspice, ground cumin, and cinnamon

Kosher salt and freshly ground black pepper

Wine pairing: Sauvignon Blanc

grilled pork with plum salsa

Serves 6

1 pork tenderloin (about 1 pound)

¼ cup dry red wine

2 tablespoons freshly squeezed orange juice

2 tablespoons olive oil

1 tablespoon honey

1 teaspoon ground cumin

Plum Salsa

1 navel orange

1 pound fresh plums or nectarines, pitted and diced

⅓ cup finely chopped red onion

1 teaspoon minced serrano chile

1 tablespoon minced fresh cilantro

1 tablespoon freshly squeezed lime juice

2 teaspoons grated fresh ginger

¼ teaspoon ground cumin

Pinch of ground cinnamon

Kosher salt and freshly ground black pepper

Wine pairing: Riesling or Zinfandel

Trim away any excess fat or silver skin from the pork and place the meat in a heavy, resealable plastic bag.

In a small bowl, whisk together the wine, orange juice, olive oil, honey, and cumin. Pour over the pork, turning to coat evenly. Seal the bag and refrigerate for at least 2 hours or up to 4 hours, turning frequently.

For the salsa: Cut the peel and pith away from the orange, following the curve of the fruit with your knife, and then cut the flesh into ½-inch cubes, discarding any seeds or large bits of membrane. Put in a glass or stainless-steel bowl. Add the plums or nectarines, onion, chile, cilantro, lime juice, ginger, cumin, and cinnamon. Season with salt and pepper. Let stand at room temperature for 1 hour, stirring often.

Remove the pork from the refrigerator at least 20 minutes before grilling. Remove the pork from the marinade and pat dry, discarding the marinade. Season with salt and pepper.

Preheat a gas grill to medium-high. Brush the grill grids with oil. Place the pork in the center of the grill, cover, and cook, turning 2 to 3 times, until an instant-read thermometer inserted in the center of the pork registers 140°F, 12 to 18 minutes. Transfer to a plate or cutting board and let stand for 10 minutes.

Cut the meat into thin slices and divide among 6 small plates. Pour any juices that have collected in the plate over the meat. Top each serving with a generous spoonful of the salsa.

flank steak with pepper crust

Serves 6

Put the steak in a heavy, resealable plastic bag. In a small bowl, combine the vinegar, soy sauce, wine, 1 teaspoon of the pepper, the garlic, and thyme. Pour over the steak and turn to coat evenly. Seal the bag and refrigerate for 8 hours, turning the bag occasionally.

Remove the meat from the refrigerator. Remove the steak from the marinade and wipe dry with a paper towel. Discard the marinade. Spread half the mustard over each side of the meat. Press half of the remaining 1 tablespoon pepper into the mustard on each side.

Preheat a gas grill to high. Oil the grill grids. Place the steak on the grill and cook for about 5 minutes on each side for medium-rare. An instant-read thermometer inserted sideways into the steak should register 125°F. Transfer to a cutting board and let rest for 10 minutes.

Cut the steak into thin slices against the grain. Arrange the arugula or watercress in small piles on 6 small plates. Divide the steak slices over the beds of greens, sprinkle with salt, and serve.

1 flank steak (1½ pounds)

¼ cup balsamic vinegar

3 tablespoons soy sauce

2 tablespoons dry red wine

1 teaspoon, plus 1 tablespoon cracked pepper

2 teaspoons minced garlic

1 teaspoon minced fresh thyme

1 tablespoon honey mustard

3 cups loosely packed arugula or watercress sprigs

Kosher or sea salt

Wine pairing: Syrah

grilled beef tenderloin
and heirloom tomato skewers

Serves 6

12 small (1-inch-diameter) Yukon Gold potatoes

One 12-ounce beef tenderloin filet, cut into 12 chunks

12 grape tomatoes

2 tablespoons olive oil

Tarragon Aioli

2 large egg yolks at room temperature

1½ teaspoons Dijon mustard

1 tablespoon freshly squeezed lemon juice

1 teaspoon minced garlic

½ to ¾ cup canola oil

2 tablespoons minced fresh tarragon

Kosher salt and freshly ground black pepper

Kosher salt and freshly ground black pepper

Wine pairing: Cabernet Sauvignon or Meritage

Soak twelve 6-inch-long bamboo skewers in water for 20 minutes.

Meanwhile, put the potatoes in a medium saucepan and add salted water to cover. Bring to a boil over high heat. Reduce the heat to a simmer and cook until just tender, 10 to 15 minutes. Be careful not to overcook. Drain.

Combine the potatoes, beef, tomatoes, and olive oil in a large bowl. Toss to coat evenly. Thread 1 chunk of meat, 1 potato, and 1 tomato onto each skewer, piercing the tomatoes lengthwise. Set aside.

For the aioli: In a blender or food processor, puree the egg yolks, mustard, lemon juice, and garlic until smooth. With the machine running, gradually add just enough canola oil in a slow, steady stream until the mixture is thick and emulsified. Stir in the tarragon. Season with salt and pepper to taste.

Preheat a gas grill to medium-high. Season the skewers with salt and pepper. Place on the grill, cover, and cook until seared, 1 to 2 minutes on each side. Arrange 2 skewers on each of 6 small plates. Serve with the aioli in small bowls on each plate.

Preheat the oven to 200°F. In a large, heavy skillet, melt 1 tablespoon of the butter over medium-high heat. Add the mushrooms and season with salt and pepper. Cook until browned, about 5 minutes. Transfer to a bowl and set aside.

Wipe out the skillet and return to medium-high heat. Add 1 tablespoon of the butter and the olive oil. Pat the steak dry, sprinkle generously with salt and pepper, and add to the skillet. Cook until seared, 3 to 4 minutes on each side. Wrap the steak loosely in aluminum foil and put in the oven to keep warm.

Discard any fat from the skillet without scraping the sides or bottom. Add 1 tablespoon of the butter and melt over low heat. Add the shallots and garlic and cook until the garlic begins to brown, about 3 minutes. Increase the heat to high. Stir in the wine and vinegar, scraping the bottom of the pan. Bring to a boil and cook until reduced to about 1/3 cup, 8 to 10 minutes. Add the stock and bring to a boil. Cook until reduced by half, 8 to 10 minutes. Stir in the basil, oregano, and mushrooms with any juices that have collected in the bowl. Reduce the heat to low and add the remaining 1 tablespoon butter in small pieces. Swirl the pan gently while the butter melts. Do not stir or whisk. Season to taste with salt and pepper to taste.

Remove the steak from the oven and transfer to a cutting board. Cut into thin slices against the grain. Divide the steak among 6 small plates and top each with a spoonful of the mushroom sauce. Serve.

seared steak with mushroom pan sauce

Serves 6

4 tablespoons unsalted butter

4 ounces shiitake mushrooms, stemmed and quartered

Kosher salt and freshly ground black pepper

1 tablespoon olive oil

1½-pound boneless New York or rib-eye steak, about 1 inch thick, trimmed

2 tablespoons minced shallots

3 cloves garlic, minced

¾ cup dry red wine

¼ cup balsamic vinegar

1 cup beef stock

1 tablespoon minced fresh basil

1 tablespoon minced fresh oregano

Wine pairing: Pinot Noir or Meritage

pepper salami skewers
with wine-poached olives and figs

Serves 6

3 large or 6 small dried black mission figs

½ cup Zinfandel or other dry red wine

6 large kalamata olives, pitted and halved lengthwise

Twelve ½-inch cubes black pepper salami

Twelve ½-inch cubes mezzo seco jack cheese or

    good-quality imported provolone

Wine pairing: Zinfandel or Syrah

If the figs are large, cut them in quarters lengthwise; if small, cut in half lengthwise. Put in a small saucepan. Add the wine and olives. Bring to a simmer over medium-low heat and cook for 10 minutes. Remove from heat, drain in a colander, and let cool.

To assemble the skewers, thread 1 piece of fig, salami, olive, and cheese onto each of twelve 6-inch bamboo skewers. Arrange on a platter or place 2 on each of 6 small plates and serve.

prosciutto and parmesan—topped bruschetta

Serves 6

Preheat the oven to 350°F. In a small bowl, cream the butter with a wooden spoon until light and creamy. Stir in the prosciutto and Parmesan. Set aside.

Arrange the bread slices on baking sheets in a single layer and bake until lightly toasted, 8 to 10 minutes. Remove from the oven. While still warm, spread 1 teaspoon of the butter over each slice. Sprinkle with the pine nuts and pepper. Arrange on a large platter or divide among 6 small plates and serve.

4 tablespoons unsalted butter at room temperature

¼ cup finely chopped prosciutto

¼ cup freshly grated Parmesan cheese

Twenty-four ½-inch-thick slices sweet baguette

⅓ cup pine nuts, toasted (see page 21)

Freshly ground black pepper

Wine pairing: Chardonnay

middle eastern mini lamb burgers

Serves 6

Lamb Burgers

12 ounces ground lamb

2 tablespoons minced fresh mint

2 tablespoons minced fresh cilantro

1½ tablespoons minced fresh oregano

2 teaspoons minced garlic

1½ teaspoons sherry vinegar

1 teaspoon light molasses

¾ teaspoon ground cumin

¼ teaspoon red pepper flakes

½ teaspoon kosher salt

¼ teaspoon freshly ground black pepper

Pinch of ground allspice

6 mini (about 4 inches in diameter) pita pockets, or

    3 regular-size pitas, halved crosswise

1 cup thinly shredded red cabbage, cut into 1-inch pieces

1 cup loosely packed fresh flat-leaf parsley leaves

½ cup (2½ ounces) crumbled feta cheese

2 tablespoons minced fresh mint

2 tablespoons sherry vinegar

1 tablespoon extra-virgin olive oil

Kosher salt and freshly ground black pepper

Wine pairing: Rosé

(continued on next page)

For the lamb burgers: In a medium bowl, combine the lamb, mint, cilantro, oregano, garlic, sherry vinegar, molasses, cumin, red pepper flakes, salt, pepper, and allspice. Shape into 6 patties, each about ½ inch thick.

Cut the top off each small pita pocket. Set aside. In a medium bowl, combine the cabbage, parsley, feta, and mint.

In a small bowl, whisk together the sherry vinegar and the olive oil. Pour over the cabbage mixture and toss to coat evenly. Season with salt and pepper to taste.

Preheat a gas grill to medium. Oil the grill grids. Place the patties on the grill and cook until browned, 3 to 4 minutes on each side. Transfer to a plate. Put the pitas on the grill and cook until lightly toasted, about 30 seconds on each side. Slide equal amounts of the cabbage mixture into each pocket and add a burger. Divide among 6 small plates and serve immediately.

lamb-filled roasted onions

Serves 6

6 tablespoons fresh bread crumbs

6 unpeeled sweet onions (8 to 10 ounces each)

1½ cups chicken stock or low-sodium broth

¼ cup dried sour cherries, coarsely chopped

1 teaspoon grated orange zest

2 tablespoons unsalted butter

12 ounces ground lamb

1 tablespoon minced fresh thyme

1 tablespoon minced fresh mint

½ teaspoon ground cinnamon

Kosher salt and freshly ground black pepper

Wine pairing: Pinot Noir or Merlot

Preheat the oven to 400°F. Spread the bread crumbs on a sided baking sheet. Bake, stirring occasionally, until lightly toasted, 3 to 5 minutes. Remove from the oven.

Cut ½ inch off the top of each onion and set the tops aside. Do not peel the onions. Cut a thin slice off the bottom, if necessary, so that each onion can stand upright. Using a paring knife, cut out the center of each onion, leaving the 2 outermost layers in place. Finely chop enough of the onion centers to make 1 cup (reserve the remainder for another use).

In a small saucepan, bring 1 cup of the stock to a boil over high heat. Cook until reduced to about ⅓ cup, 7 to 10 minutes. Add the cherries and orange zest. Remove from the heat, cover, and let stand.

In a large skillet, melt 1 tablespoon of the butter over medium heat. Add the chopped onion and cook until tender, about 5 minutes. Add the lamb and cook, stirring often to break up the meat, until browned, 6 to 8 minutes. Remove from the heat. Stir in the cherry mixture, thyme, mint, and cinnamon. Season with salt and pepper to taste.

Spoon an equal amount of the filling into the center of each onion and place in a baking dish. Pour the remaining ½ cup stock into the baking dish. Top each onion with first 1 tablespoon of bread crumbs followed by a small piece of the remaining 1 tablespoon of butter. Place the onion tops in the baking dish but not on top of the onions and bake, uncovered, for 20 minutes. Cover with aluminum foil and bake until tender, about 30 minutes. Remove the foil and bake until crumbs are crisp and browned, about 5 minutes. Replace the onion tops. Divide the onions among 6 small plates and serve.

duck and spinach empanadas with persimmon chutney

Serves 6

Chutney

1 pound firm, ripe Fuyu persimmons or nectarines,

    peeled and diced

2 tablespoons honey

1 tablespoon freshly squeezed lemon juice

1 tablespoon minced fresh ginger

3 tablespoons sliced almonds, toasted (see page 21)

¼ teaspoon almond extract

Empanadas

4 ounces thawed frozen spinach (half of one 10-ounce package)

1 tablespoon extra-virgin olive oil

¼ cup finely chopped red onion

¼ cup finely chopped red bell pepper

2 cloves garlic, minced

3 tablespoons dry sherry

2 tablespoons golden raisins, chopped

¾ cup shredded cooked duck, chicken, or turkey meat

Kosher salt and freshly ground black pepper

1 package (2 crusts) refrigerated pie pastry

1 large egg, beaten

Wine pairing: Riesling or Syrah

(continued on next page)

duck and spinach empanadas
with persimmon chutney continued

For the chutney: In a small saucepan, combine the persimmons, honey, lemon juice, and ginger. Bring to a boil over medium heat. Reduce the heat to low and simmer, stirring frequently, until the persimmons are soft, about 5 minutes. Remove from the heat and stir in the almonds and almond extract. Let cool. (This can be made in advance and refrigerated for up to 1 week.)

For the empanadas: Drain the spinach. Firmly squeeze to remove any excess liquid, then chop.

In a large skillet, heat the olive oil over medium-high heat. Add the onion, bell pepper, and garlic. Cook until the onion is soft, 3 to 5 minutes. Add the sherry and raisins. Increase the heat to high, bring to a boil, and cook, stirring often, until the sherry is nearly evaporated, about 2 minutes. Remove from the heat and stir in the spinach and meat. Season with salt and pepper to taste.

Transfer 1 pie dough round to a lightly floured board and roll out to thin slightly. Cut the dough into 9 circles with a 3-inch round cookie cutter. Repeat with the remaining dough round. Place 1 scant tablespoon of filling in the center of each circle, then fold the pastry over, brush the edges with egg, and press together with a fork to seal. Arrange on a baking sheet lined with parchment paper and refrigerate for 30 minutes.

Preheat the oven to 375°F. Brush the top of the empanadas with the remaining egg. Bake until the pastry is golden, 18 to 20 minutes. Remove from the oven and arrange on a large serving platter or divide among 6 small plates. Serve with the chutney alongside.

pork saltimbocca with pan sauce

Serves 6

Season the pork on both sides with salt and pepper. Put a prosciutto slice on a work surface. Place a pork cutlet or chop in the center. Wrap the ends of the prosciutto around the pork, overlapping in the center. Place a sage leaf over the ends and thread an 8-inch bamboo skewer through the pork to secure the prosciutto and sage. Repeat with the remaining pork cutlets or chops.

In a large skillet, melt the butter with the oil over medium-high heat. Add the cutlets or chops, in batches if necessary, sage side down, in a single layer and cook until the prosciutto is crisp and the pork is lightly browned on the bottom, about 3 minutes. Turn and cook the second side for 2 minutes. Transfer to a plate and cover with aluminum foil to keep warm.

Discard any oil from the skillet and add the wine. Increase the heat to high and cook until thickened, stirring to scrape up the browned bits on the bottom of the pan, about 3 minutes. Arrange the pork on a platter or divide among 6 small plates, spoon the pan sauce over each, and serve.

6 small (about 3 ounces each) boneless pork cutlets or thin-cut pork chops, trimmed

Kosher salt and freshly ground black pepper

6 thin slices prosciutto

6 small fresh sage leaves

2 tablespoons unsalted butter

2 tablespoons olive oil

½ cup dry white wine

Wine pairing: Chardonnay or Pinot Noir

braised chicken with swiss chard

Serves 6

1 large bunch Swiss chard, rinsed and dried

2 slices bacon, diced

6 chicken thighs

Kosher salt and freshly ground black pepper

1 carrot, peeled and finely diced

1 stalk celery, finely diced

1 shallot, minced

3 thyme sprigs

½ cup dry red wine

1 cup chicken stock or low-sodium broth

1 tablespoon Dijon mustard

2 tablespoons unsalted butter

3 tablespoons minced fresh flat-leaf parsley

Wine pairing: Pinot Noir or Cabernet Sauvignon

Hold a stalk of Swiss chard and slide your other hand along the stalk, stripping away the leaf. Repeat with all of the leaves. Trim away the bottom of the stalks and cut the stalks into ½-inch-thick slices. Cut the leaves into 1-inch pieces. Set aside.

In a skillet just large enough to hold all the chicken pieces in a single layer, fry the bacon over medium-low heat, stirring occasionally, until crisp, about 7 minutes. Using a slotted spoon, transfer to paper towels to drain. Increase the heat under the skillet to medium-high.

Season the chicken liberally with salt and pepper and add to the skillet, skin side down. Cook until browned, about 4 minutes on each side. Using tongs, transfer to a plate.

Add the Swiss chard stalks to the skillet and cook until softened, about 3 minutes. Using a slotted spoon, transfer to a plate. Add the carrot, celery, half of the shallot, and the thyme sprigs to the skillet. Cook until the vegetables are softened, about 5 minutes. Add the wine and cook until nearly dry, about 5 minutes. Add the stock and bring to a boil. Add the chicken, skin side up. Cover with a lid slightly askew and reduce the heat to medium. Cook until the chicken is opaque throughout, about 20 minutes. Using a slotted metal spatula, transfer the chicken to a plate.

Remove the thyme sprigs from the pan and whisk in the mustard. Stir in the Swiss chard leaves and cook until wilted. Stir in the Swiss chard stalks, the butter, and 2 tablespoons of the parsley. Season with salt and pepper to taste. Divide the Swiss chard among 6 shallow bowls or small plates and place a piece of chicken on top. Sprinkle with the bacon and the remaining parsley and serve.

desserts

warm chocolate puddle cakes

Makes 6 cakes

Preheat the oven to 400°F. Heavily butter and lightly flour six 4- to 6-ounce ramekins. Knock out the excess flour.

In a double boiler over simmering water, melt the butter and chocolate. Remove from the heat and set aside.

In a large bowl, whisk together the eggs, egg yolks, and the ⅓ cup sugar. Stir in the 1 tablespoon coffee liqueur. Whisk in the chocolate mixture, then fold in the flour. Divide the batter evenly among the ramekins. Place the ramekins on a baking sheet and bake until firm at the edges and glossy and barely set in the center, 9 to 11 minutes. Remove from the oven and let cool for 10 minutes in the pan.

In a deep bowl, beat the cream until soft peaks form. Add additional sugar and coffee liqueur to taste.

Run a sharp knife around the edges of the cakes to loosen them. Invert each cake onto one of 6 small plates and top each with a dollop of the whipped cream.

6 tablespoons unsalted butter

8 ounces semisweet chocolate, chopped

2 large eggs

2 large egg yolks

⅓ cup sugar, plus additional sugar

1 tablespoon coffee liqueur, plus additional liqueur

⅓ cup all-purpose flour

½ cup heavy cream

Wine pairing: Port

apple dumplings

Makes 6 dumplings

6 small (2½ inches wide) Fuji apples, peeled

¼ cup walnuts, toasted (see page 21)

5 tablespoons unsalted butter at room temperature

¼ cup packed brown sugar

½ teaspoon vanilla extract

½ teaspoon ground ginger

½ teaspoon ground cinnamon

Pinch of salt

Pastry Dough (page 127)

1 large egg, lightly beaten

Raw sugar for sprinkling

Wine pairing: Late Harvest Chardonnay

Core the apples, leaving the base intact. If necessary, cut a thin slice from the bottom of each apple so it will stand upright.

In a food processor, pulse the walnuts until chopped. Add the butter, brown sugar, vanilla, ginger, cinnamon, and salt and process until blended. Stuff equal amounts of the nut mixture into the center of each apple. Place the apples on a plate, cover, and refrigerate until the butter mixture is firm, about 30 minutes.

Preheat the oven to 375°F. Line a rimmed baking sheet with parchment paper.

On a floured board, roll out 1 piece of dough into a 6-inch round disk, about ⅛ inch thick. Place an apple in the center and pull the dough up around the apple, creating a seal at the top by pleating and pinching the dough together. Repeat with the remaining dough and apples. Brush with the beaten egg and arrange on the prepared pan. Sprinkle with raw sugar. Bake until the apple is tender and the pastry is browned (the dumplings may leak slightly), 40 to 45 minutes. Remove from the oven and let cool for 20 minutes. Carefully transfer each dumpling to a small plate and serve.

Preheat the oven to 325°F. Butter and flour 6 nonstick muffin cups; knock out the excess flour.

In the bowl of a stand mixer fitted with the paddle attachment, combine the almond paste, butter, and the ¼ cup sugar. Beat on medium speed until smooth and creamy. Add the eggs one at a time, beating after each addition. Add the liqueur and mix until incorporated.

In a medium bowl, combine the flour, baking powder, and salt. Stir with a whisk to blend. Fold into the almond mixture until blended. Divide the batter among the prepared muffin cups. Bake until a toothpick inserted in the center of a cake comes out clean, 25 to 30 minutes. Remove from the oven and let cool in the pan for 10 minutes. Unmold onto a wire rack and let cool completely.

Cut the cakes in half crosswise to create 2 layers. Spread equal amounts of the jam over the bottom half of each cake. Replace the tops. In a deep bowl, beat the cream and the 1 teaspoon sugar together until soft peaks form. Top each cupcake with a dollop of whipped cream and several raspberries. Place each cake on a small decorative plate and serve.

almond layer cakes with raspberries and jam

Makes six 3-inch cakes

One 7-ounce package almond paste

6 tablespoons unsalted butter at room temperature

¼ cup sugar, plus 1 teaspoon

2 large eggs

2 teaspoons orange liqueur, such as

Grand Marnier or Cointreau

½ cup all-purpose flour

½ teaspoon baking powder

¼ teaspoon salt

2 tablespoons raspberry jam

⅓ cup heavy cream

1 cup fresh raspberries

Wine pairing: Muscat Canelli or Late Harvest Chardonnay

plum crostadas

Makes six 4-inch tarts

Cornmeal Pastry Dough

1¼ cups all-purpose flour

¼ cup cornmeal

½ teaspoon kosher salt

½ cup (1 stick) cold unsalted butter, cut into pieces

3 tablespoons sour cream

4 to 5 tablespoons ice water

Syrup

½ cup sugar

½ cup dry white wine

¼ cup water

1 teaspoon balsamic vinegar

1 sprig rosemary

One ½-inch-wide strip lemon zest

½ bay leaf

10 peppercorns

1 pound ripe but firm plums, pitted and cut

    into ⅛-inch-thick slices

1 large egg, lightly beaten

2 tablespoons raw sugar

Wine pairing: Muscat Canelli or Late Harvest Chardonnay

For the dough: In a food processor, combine the flour, cornmeal, and salt. Pulse until combined. Add the butter and pulse until the mixture is crumbly and the butter is the size of small peas. Add the sour cream and pulse to combine. Add the water, 1 tablespoon at a time, and pulse just until the dough begins to form a ball. On a lightly floured board, form the dough into a ball, divide into 6 portions, and shape each into a disk. Wrap in plastic wrap and refrigerate for 30 minutes.

(continued on next page)

plum crostadas continued

For the syrup: In a small saucepan, combine the sugar, wine, water, vinegar, rosemary, lemon zest, bay leaf, and peppercorns. Bring to a boil over medium heat, reduce the heat to a simmer, and cook until reduced and thickened to a syrup, 25 to 30 minutes. Remove from the heat and let cool. Strain through a fine-meshed sieve into a sealable container.

Preheat the oven to 375°F. Line a baking sheet with parchment paper.

On a floured board, roll out each pastry disk into a 6-inch round, about ¼ inch thick, and place on the prepared pan. Arrange an equal amount of plum slices in concentric circles in the center of each disk, leaving a 1-inch border. Fold the border over the plums, pleating as you go. Brush each pastry with the egg. Sprinkle each with about 1 teaspoon of the raw sugar and bake until the pastry is golden brown, about 30 minutes. Remove from the oven and transfer to wire racks. Let cool completely.

Arrange the crostadas on a platter or divide among 6 small plates and drizzle with the rosemary syrup. Serve.

mini summer squash cupcakes with lemon glaze

Makes 18 mini cupcakes

½ cup all-purpose flour

2 tablespoons almond flour (almond meal)

½ teaspoon baking powder

Pinch of salt

4 tablespoons unsalted butter at room temperature

⅓ cup granulated sugar

1 large egg

½ teaspoon vanilla extract

½ teaspoon grated lemon zest

6 tablespoons buttermilk

¾ cup shredded yellow zucchini or summer squash

¾ cup confectioners' sugar

1 to 2 tablespoons freshly squeezed lemon juice

1 tablespoon lemon zest cut into fine slivers, for garnish

Wine pairing: Muscat Canelli or Late Harvest Chardonnay

Preheat the oven to 350°F. Butter and flour 18 mini-muffin cups. Knock out the excess flour.

In a small bowl, combine the flour, almond flour, baking powder, and salt. Stir with a whisk to blend.

In a large bowl, combine the butter and granulated sugar using an electric beater on medium-low speed. Add the egg, vanilla, and lemon zest and beat until blended. Add half of the flour mixture, then half of the buttermilk, adding each after the last is completely incorporated. Repeat with the remaining flour mixture and buttermilk.

Place the shredded zucchini or squash in a tea towel, roll up, and squeeze firmly to wring out the excess moisture. Stir into the batter. Spoon into the prepared muffin cups, leaving ¼ inch of space at the top of each cup. Bake until a toothpick inserted into the center of a cupcake comes out clean, 25 to 30 minutes. Remove from the oven and let cool in the pan for 10 minutes. Unmold onto a wire rack set over a sheet of parchment or waxed paper. Let cool completely.

In a small bowl, stir together the confectioners' sugar and lemon juice. Spoon the glaze over the cupcakes and garnish with the lemon zest slivers. Let stand until set, 1 to 2 hours.

Arrange on a platter or place 3 cupcakes on each of 6 small plates and serve.

dark chocolate truffles

Makes 22 truffles

In a heavy, medium-size saucepan, combine the cream, vanilla, and salt. Bring to a boil over medium-low heat. Stir in the wine.

Remove from the heat and stir in the chopped chocolate until completely melted. Stir in the butter until it melts and is completely incorporated into the chocolate. Pour into a container, cover, and refrigerate until firm, at least 2 hours.

Line 2 baking sheets with parchment paper. Using a teaspoon or melon baller (dipped in hot water and dried), shape the chocolate into 1-inch balls. Place on the prepared baking sheets. Refrigerate for 10 minutes.

Spread the cocoa powder on a rimmed plate. Roll the truffle balls gently between your hands to shape into smooth round balls. Roll each truffle in cocoa powder. Dust 6 small plates with cocoa powder or confectioners' sugar. Arrange 3 or 4 truffles on each plate and serve.

1/3 cup heavy cream

1/2 teaspoon vanilla extract

Scant pinch of salt

2 tablespoons Cabernet Sauvignon wine

6 ounces high-quality semisweet or bittersweet chocolate, chopped

1 tablespoon unsalted butter at room temperature

1/4 cup high-quality unsweetened cocoa powder, plus more for dusting

Confectioners' sugar, for dusting

Wine pairing: Cabernet Sauvignon or Meritage

bite-size brownies with chocolate-cabernet glaze

Makes thirty-six 1-inch brownies

¾ cup Cabernet Sauvignon or other dry red wine

⅔ cup all-purpose flour

⅔ cup high-quality unsweetened cocoa powder

¼ teaspoon salt

½ cup (1 stick) unsalted butter at room temperature

1 cup sugar

1 large egg

1 large egg yolk

1 teaspoon vanilla extract

¼ cup heavy cream

½ cup semisweet chocolate chips

Wine pairing: Port or Cabernet Sauvignon

Preheat the oven to 350°F. Butter the bottom and sides of an 8-inch square baking dish, then line with crossed sheets of parchment paper to completely cover the bottom and sides. Lightly butter the parchment paper.

In a small saucepan, bring the wine to a boil over high heat. Cook until reduced to ⅓ cup, about 10 minutes. Remove and reserve 1 tablespoon for the icing.

In a small bowl, combine the flour, cocoa powder, and salt. Stir with a whisk to blend. In a medium bowl, cream the butter and sugar until light and fluffy.

In a medium bowl, whisk together the reduced wine, egg, egg yolk, and ¾ teaspoon of the vanilla. Stir into the butter mixture. Stir in the flour mixture, blending only until incorporated. Spread evenly in the prepared baking dish. Bake until a toothpick inserted into the center comes out almost clean, about 25 minutes. Remove from the oven and let cool completely on a wire rack.

In a small saucepan, heat the cream over medium heat until tiny bubbles begin to form around the edge. Remove from the heat and stir in the chocolate chips until melted. Whisk in the reserved tablespoon of reduced wine and the remaining ¼ teaspoon vanilla. Let cool slightly.

Remove the brownies from the pan, peel away the parchment paper, and spread the melted chocolate mixture over the top. Refrigerate until the glaze is set, about 1 hour. Transfer to a cutting board and, using a large knife, trim away the uneven edges, then cut the brownies into 36 small squares. Arrange 3 squares on each of 6 small plates and serve.

caramel nut tartlets

Makes six 4-inch tartlets

Pastry Dough

1½ cups all-purpose flour

2 tablespoons sugar

¼ teaspoon salt

10 tablespoons cold unsalted butter, cut into ½-inch pieces

1 large egg yolk

3 to 5 tablespoons ice water

Filling

⅓ cup packed brown sugar

⅓ cup granulated sugar

2 tablespoons water

1 tablespoon corn syrup

½ cup heavy cream

1 tablespoon unsalted butter

1 cup mixed nuts, such as pine nuts, sliced almonds,

    chopped pecans, or chopped walnuts

Wine pairing: Late Harvest Chardonnay

Cut six 6-inch squares of aluminum foil.

For the dough: In a food processor, combine the flour, sugar, and salt. Pulse to blend. Add the butter and pulse until the mixture resembles coarse crumbs. Add the egg yolk and process for a few seconds, then add the ice water, 1 tablespoon at a time, and pulse until the dough just begins to come together in a ball.

On a floured board, form the dough into a ball, divide into 6 pieces, then form each into a disk. Wrap each in plastic wrap and chill for at least 30 minutes or up to 24 hours.

Preheat the oven to 400°F. On a floured surface, roll each dough disk into a 6-inch round. Fit each into a 4-inch fluted tart pan ¾ inch high. Trim away any dough overhanging the edge with a sharp knife. Fit a square of aluminum foil carefully into each tart shell and fill with pie weights or dried beans. Place the pans on a baking sheet and bake for 15 minutes. Carefully remove the foil and weights, prick the bottom of the pastry, return to the oven, and bake until the pastry appears dry and is golden brown on the edges, 8 to 10 minutes longer. Remove from the oven and let cool on a wire rack.

For the filling: In a medium, heavy saucepan, combine the brown sugar, granulated sugar, water, and corn syrup. Heat over medium heat, stirring until the sugar dissolves. Continue to cook without stirring, swirling the pan by the handle occasionally, until

(continued on next page)

the mixture reaches 300°F on a candy thermometer (tilt the pan if necessary to get an accurate reading), 7 to 10 minutes. Remove from the heat. Gradually pour in the cream, stirring carefully, as the mixture will boil up and release steam. Stir in the butter, again being careful to avoid any spatters. Cook over low heat, stirring, until smooth, about 5 minutes. Stir in the nuts.

Divide the filling evenly among the 6 tart shells. Place the tart pans on a baking sheet and bake until the pastry is a slightly deeper golden brown, about 10 minutes. Remove from the oven, place on wire racks, and let cool completely. Divide among 6 small plates and serve.

putting it all together: small-plates menus

Like a well-made dish, a really good menu will also have balance.

—Justin Wangler, Kendall-Jackson executive chef

One of the major charms of small plates is they are meant to be mixed and matched, and you can combine as few or as many as you like. You can create a menu based on the season, your favorite wine varietal, or your favorite type of cuisine. Dishes can be served in courses, or all at once.

The best menus include at least three or four different dishes, offer a variety of vegetables and protein, include a selection of textures, and provide contrast between warm and cold dishes. As for wine, the best menus fit your taste and style. Feeling adventurous? Offer a different wine with each individual recipe. Want to keep it as simple as possible? Select one wine for each course, or one varietal for the entire menu.

The menus that follow were created to reflect a season or occasion. Most are designed to be served in courses, but would be equally delicious served all together. Each suggests one or more wine varietals to try with each course. For courses that include more than one dish, one or all of the varietals suggested can be served. Use these menus as a guide for creating fabulous meals, or let them inspire you to assemble your own unforgettable combinations of small plates.

spring celebration

preparation plan:

4 Hours Ahead:
Bake the cakes
Cook the asparagus and tie into bundles
Select serving plates, bowls, and serving pieces
Chill white wine
Bake the beets

2 Hours Ahead:
Assemble the cakes
Whip the cream for the cakes and refrigerate
Make the date vinaigrette
Prepare the asparagus topping

1 Hour Ahead:
Prepare the orange-fennel mixture for the rock shrimp salad
Make the couscous for the tuna
Set the table

When Ready to Serve:
Toss the beets with the vinaigrette
Bake the asparagus with the Brie, finish, and serve
Cook the rock shrimp, add to the salad, and serve
Sear the tuna, slice, and serve over the couscous
Serve the beets with the tuna
Top the cakes with the whipped cream and serve

backyard cookout

Suggested Serving Order:

Prawn Skewers with Lime Marinade (page 64)
Wine: Riesling or Rosé

Mediterranean Cucumber Salad (page 22)
Wine: Sauvignon Blanc

Grilled Eggplant–Red Pepper Rolls (page 44)

Middle Eastern Mini Lamb Burgers (page 96)
    or
Flank Steak with Pepper Crust (page 87)
Wine: Pinot Noir, Merlot, or Cabernet Sauvignon

Plum Crostadas (page 118)
Wine: Muscat Canelli or Late Harvest Chardonnay

preparation plan:

8 Hours Ahead:
Prepare the steak marinade, pour over the meat, and refrigerate

4 Hours Ahead:
Prepare the marinade for the prawns, pour over the prawns,
    and refrigerate
Prepare the garlic oil and grill the eggplant and red peppers for
    the rolls

Make the dough for the crostadas and refrigerate
Make the syrup for the crostadas
Select serving plates, bowls, and serving utensils
Chill white wine (reds too, if the weather is really hot)

2 Hours Ahead:
Mix the ingredients for the lamb burgers and make patties
Roll out the dough, assemble, and bake the crostadas
Make the vinaigrette for the cucumber salad
Prepare the vegetables for the cucumber salad
Remove the steak from the refrigerator

1 Hour Ahead:
Soak the skewers for the prawns
Combine the cucumber salad and vinaigrette
Combine the ingredients for the lamb burger–cabbage mixture
Make the filling for the eggplant rolls and assemble rolls
Thread the prawns onto the skewers
Set the table

20 Minutes Ahead:
Preheat a gas grill to medium-high heat

When Ready to Serve:
Grill the prawns and serve
Arrange the eggplant and red pepper rolls on serving plates
Grill the lamb burgers, assemble, and serve
    or
Grill the steak, slice, and serve
Divide the cucumber salad among the serving plates, top with
    the cheese, and serve
Drizzle the crostadas with the syrup and serve

fresh from the summer garden

Suggested Serving Order:

Chilled Corn Soup with Meyer Lemon Olive Oil (page 40)
Wine: Chardonnay or Rosé

Ratatouille with Summer Herbs (page 43)

Green Beans with Lemon Vinaigrette, Blue Cheese, and Almonds
  (page 21)

Grilled Pork with Plum Salsa (page 84)
Wine: Riesling, Zinfandel, or Syrah

Mini Summer Squash Cupcakes with Lemon Glaze (page 122)
Wine: Muscat Canelli

preparation plan:

6 Hours Ahead:
Prepare the corn soup and refrigerate

4 Hours Ahead:
Prepare the pork marinade, pour over the pork, and refrigerate
Prepare and bake the squash cupcakes
Select your serving plates, bowls, and serving pieces
Chill white wine (red too, if the weather is really hot)
Prepare the lemon glaze and spread over the cupcakes

1 Hour Ahead:
Cook the green beans
Prepare the vinaigrette for the green beans
Toast the almonds for the green beans
Prepare the salsa for the pork
Set the table

20 Minutes Ahead:
Preheat a gas grill to medium-high
Remove the pork from the refrigerator

When Ready to Serve:
Toss the green beans with the vinaigrette
Grill the pork and let sit
Divide the corn soup among 6 bowls, drizzle with the oil, and serve
Divide the beans among 6 plates and top with cheese and almonds
Slice the pork, divide among 6 plates, top with the salsa, and serve
Arrange the cupcakes on a platter or on individual plates and serve

autumn harvest

Suggested Serving Order:

Caramelized Pear and Walnut Salad with Prosciutto (page 28)
Wine: Chardonnay

Balsamic-Glazed Potatoes and Onions (page 51)

Grilled Celery with Truffle Oil (page 55)

Seared Steak with Mushroom Pan Sauce (page 91)
Wine: Chardonnay or Pinot Noir

Apple Dumplings (page 114)
Wine: Late Harvest Chardonnay

preparation plan:

4 Hours Ahead:
Make the tart dough
Select serving plates, bowls, and serving pieces
Chill white wine

2 Hours Ahead:
Prepare the apple stuffing, stuff the apples, and refrigerate
Make the vinaigrette for the salad
Peel the onions for the potatoes
Bake the potatoes and keep warm

1 Hour Ahead:
Roll out the dough, assemble the apple dumplings, and bake
Prepare the celery
Gather and prepare the ingredients for the steak
Set the table

20 Minutes Ahead:
Preheat a gas grill to high heat
Assemble the potatoes in the baking dish, cover, and return
    to the oven to warm

When Ready to Serve:
Assemble the pear salad and serve
Cook the steak and mushroom sauce
Grill the celery
Serve the steak, celery, and potatoes
Serve the apple dumplings

holiday dinner party

Suggested Serving Order:

Citrus-Cured Salmon on Blini (page 76)
Wine: Sauvignon Blanc

Crab Salad with Rémoulade (page 68)
Wine: Chardonnay

Roasted Brussels Sprouts with Chorizo (page 52)
    or
Fennel and Gorgonzola Gratin (page 48)

Pork Saltimbocca with Pan Sauce (page 107)
Wine: Chardonnay, Merlot, or Pinot Noir

Warm Chocolate Puddle Cakes (page 113)
Wine: Port

preparation plan:

24 hours ahead:
Prepare the salmon cure, cover the salmon, and refrigerate

4 hours ahead:
Prepare the blini batter
Make the rémoulade for the crab salad

Select serving plates, bowls, and serving pieces
Chill white wine

2 Hours Ahead:
Assemble the pork saltimbocca
Prepare the fennel and arrange in the gratin dishes
Cook the cauliflower
Soak the raisins for the Brussels sprouts

1 Hour Ahead:
Slice the salmon
Assemble and bake the Brussels sprouts
Set the table

30 Minutes Ahead:
Cook the blini

When Ready to Serve:
Toss the cabbage for the crab salad and divide among 6 plates
Assemble the crab salad and arrange on top of the cabbage
Bake the fennel with the Gorgonzola
Assemble the blini and salmon and serve
Serve the crab salad
Cook the pork saltimbocca and sauce; serve
Serve the Brussels sprouts
Serve the fennel
Prepare and bake the chocolate puddle cakes
Whip the cream
Serve the chocolate puddle cakes

finger food only

Suggested Serving Order:

Lemon-Chicken Kebabs with Moroccan Herb Sauce (page 83)
Wine: Sauvignon Blanc

Duck and Spinach Empanadas with Persimmon Chutney (page 102)
Wine: Riesling

Golden Chanterelle–Topped Crostini (page 47)
Wine: Pinot Noir
    or
Prosciutto and Parmesan–Topped Bruschetta (page 95)
Wine: Chardonnay

Pepper Salami Skewers with Wine-Poached Olives and Figs
    (page 92)
Wine: Zinfandel

preparation plan:

24 Hours Ahead:
Make the chutney for the empanadas

4 Hours Ahead:
Make the marinade for the chicken skewers, pour over the
    chicken, and refrigerate
Make the filling for the empanadas

Bake the crostini
Poach the figs and olives for the salami skewers
Select and gather serving plates and pieces
Chill the white wine

2 Hours Ahead:
Make the herb sauce for the chicken kebabs
Assemble the empanadas

1 Hour Ahead:
Prepare the bruschetta topping

30 Minutes Ahead:
Soak the skewers
Preheat the oven
Bake the empanadas
Preheat a gas grill to medium-high heat
Assemble the salami skewers
Assemble the chicken kebabs
Prepare the chanterelles

When Ready to Serve:
Grill the chicken kebabs and serve with the herb sauce
Bake the bruschetta, assemble, and serve
Serve the empanadas with the salsa
Assemble and serve the crostini
Serve the salami skewers

desserts only

Mini Summer Squash Cupcakes with Lemon Glaze (page 122)
Wine: Muscat Canelli

Caramel Nut Tartlets (page 127)
Wine: Late Harvest Chardonnay

Dark Chocolate Truffles (page 125)
Wine: Cabernet Sauvignon

preparation plan:

4 Hours Ahead:
Make the dough for the nut tarts and refrigerate
Prepare and bake the squash cupcakes
Prepare the chocolate mixture for the truffles and refrigerate

2 Hours Ahead:
Roll out and bake the tart shells
Make the nut filling
Prepare the lemon glaze and spread over the cupcakes
Shape the truffles into balls and refrigerate

1 Hour Ahead:
Bake the nut tartlets
Coat the truffles with cocoa powder

When Ready to Serve:
Divide the tartlets, truffles, and cupcakes together equally
between 6 small plates

making small plates picture-perfect

Small plates are fun. They are fun to eat, fun to combine, and especially fun to serve. They can be served family style for casual gatherings, or each dish can be presented on individual plates or in individual bowls for more formal occasions. The latter does not necessarily require much more effort, and the results are definitely more elegant. Use the following serving ideas for making your meal look as wonderful as it tastes.

Plates
Not since formal china was *de rigueur* for table settings has there been such a great selection of plates available in a huge array of sizes. If you don't already have enough small plates to serve several dishes for a meal, or if you need ideas for adding to your stock, consider any of these types of plates:

Colorful, decorative saucers

Geometric appetizer plates

Disposable bamboo plates

Sushi plates

Bread plates from formal china sets

Bowls

There's been a recent proliferation of restaurants serving small portions of food in large, shallow bowls. The presentation is dramatic, and it's effortless. If you have a set of shallow bowls, consider using them for serving foods normally served on plates. For recipes normally served in bowls, consider these options:

Decorative espresso cups

Fancy teacups

Martini glasses

Ramekins

Finger bowls from china sets

Edible bowls such as lettuce leaves

Presentation

Cooking is a lot more than just preparing a meal; it's also an art form in which food is presented with flair. Small plates make it easy to express creativity in the way that a single dish or an entire meal is served. Consider incorporating these ideas into your next small-plates meal:

- Mix and match shapes, colors, and textures of plates and bowls.
- Stack a small plate on top of a large plate, with or without a colorful napkin in between.
- Arrange small bowls or plates on a tray and pass them as an appetizer.

- Nestle small, plain bowls inside larger, more decorative bowls.
- Fill the bottom of decorative glasses with beans and stand skewers of food in the glasses.

Finding Interesting Serving Pieces

- Big-box and 99-cent stores are great sources for inexpensive and seasonal serving pieces.
- Flea markets, estate sales, and consignment shops are treasure troves for mix-and-match china and other vintage plates and bowls.
- Restaurant supply stores have a great inventory of fun, whimsical containers, such as Chinese take-out boxes or checkered burger boxes.
- Kitchenware stores offer a large selection of items perfect for individual servings, from tiny cast-iron skillets to miniature gratin dishes.

equivalents

Metric Conversion Formulas

To Convert	Multiply
Ounces to grams	Ounces by 28.35
Pounds to kilograms	Pounds by .454
Teaspoons to milliliters	Teaspoons by 4.93
Tablespoons to milliliters	Tablespoons by 14.79
Fluid ounces to milliliters	Fluid ounces by 29.57
Cups to milliliters	Cups by 236.59
Cups to liters	Cups by .236
Pints to liters	Pints by .473
Quarts to liters	Quarts by .946
Gallons to liters	Gallons by 3.785
Inches to centimeters	Inches by 2.54

Approximate Metric Equivalents

Volume

¼ teaspoon	1 milliliter
½ teaspoon	2.5 milliliters
¾ teaspoon	4 milliliters
1 teaspoon	5 milliliters
1¼ teaspoon	6 milliliters
1½ teaspoon	7.5 milliliters
1¾ teaspoon	8.5 milliliters
2 teaspoons	10 milliliters
1 tablespoon (½ fluid ounce)	15 milliliters
2 tablespoons (1 fluid ounce)	30 milliliters
¼ cup	60 milliliters
⅓ cup	80 milliliters
½ cup (4 fluid ounces)	120 milliliters
⅔ cup	160 milliliters
¾ cup	180 milliliters
1 cup (8 fluid ounces)	240 milliliters
1¼ cups	300 milliliters
1½ cups (12 fluid ounces)	360 milliliters
1⅔ cups	400 milliliters
2 cups (1 pint)	460 milliliters
3 cups	700 milliliters
4 cups (1 quart)	0.95 liter
1 quart plus ¼ cup	1 liter
4 quarts (1 gallon)	3.8 liters

Weight

¼ ounce	7 grams
½ ounce	14 grams
¾ ounce	21 grams
1 ounce	28 grams
1¼ ounces	35 grams
1½ ounces	42.5 grams
1⅔ ounces	45 grams
2 ounces	57 grams
3 ounces	85 grams
4 ounces (¼ pound)	113 grams
5 ounces	142 grams
6 ounces	170 grams
7 ounces	198 grams
8 ounces (½ pound)	227 grams
16 ounces (1 pound)	454 grams
35.25 ounces (2.2 pounds)	1 kilogram

Length

⅛ inch	3 millimeters
¼ inch	6 millimeters
½ inch	1¼ centimeters
1 inch	2½ centimeters
2 inches	5 centimeters
2½ inches	6 centimeters
4 inches	10 centimeters
5 inches	13 centimeters
6 inches	15¼ centimeters
12 inches (1 foot)	30 centimeters

equivalents

Oven Temperatures

To convert Fahrenheit to Celsius, subtract 32 from Fahrenheit, multiply the result by 5, then divide by 9.

Description	Fahrenheit	Celsius	British Gas Mark
Very cool	200°	95°	0
Very cool	225°	110°	¼
Very cool	250°	120°	½
Cool	275°	135°	1
Cool	300°	150°	2
Warm	325°	165°	3
Moderate	350°	175°	4
Moderately hot	375°	190°	5
Fairly hot	400°	200°	6
Hot	425°	220°	7
Very hot	450°	230°	8
Very hot	475°	245°	9

Common Ingredients and Their Approximate Equivalents

1 cup uncooked rice = 225 grams

1 cup all-purpose flour = 140 grams

1 stick butter (4 ounces • ½ cup • 8 tablespoons) = 110 grams

1 cup butter (8 ounces • 2 sticks • 16 tablespoons) = 220 grams

1 cup brown sugar, firmly packed = 225 grams

1 cup granulated sugar = 200 grams

Information compiled from a variety of sources, including *Recipes into Type* by Joan Whitman and Dolores Simon (Newton, MA: Biscuit Books, 2000); *The New Food Lover's Companion* by Sharon Tyler Herbst (Hauppauge, NY: Barron's, 1995); and *Rosemary Brown's Big Kitchen Instruction Book* (Kansas City, MO: Andrews McMeel, 1998).

acknowledgments

This book was a fun adventure made so by the amazing team with whom I had the pleasure of working, including Ruth Souroujon and George Rose of Kendall-Jackson, my longtime friends who invited me to work on this project; publisher Kirsty Melville and senior editor Jean Lucas at Andrews McMeel Publishers, whose support of the book and gentle guidance made its publication possible; winemaker Randy Ullom, executive chef Justin Wangler, and the unbeatable culinary team at Kendall-Jackson; Kate Washington, who tested every recipe; copyeditor Carolyn Miller, who made sure every "T" was crossed; photographer Dan Mills and stylists Kim Konecny and Julia Scahill, who made each dish look so beautiful on the page; Damon Campolo and Jay Desai for their time and gracious assistance during the photo shoot; and especially Jennifer Barry, who conceived of the project and whose design abilities are rivaled only by her awesome ability to see the big picture and bring it to life.

index